LAST LETTER
TO A READER

Last Letter
to a Reader

GERALD MURNANE

SHEFFIELD – LONDON – NEW YORK

And Other Stories
Sheffield – London – New York
www.andotherstories.org

Originally published in 2021 by Giramondo, Australia

1 3 5 7 9 8 6 4 2

ISBN: 9781913505424
eBook ISBN: 9781913505431

Typesetter: Tetragon, London; Typefaces: Albertan Pro and
Linotype Syntax; Cover Design:Sarahmay Wilkinson. Printed and
bound by the CPI Group (UK) Ltd, Croydon CRO 4YY.

A catalogue record for this book is available from the British Library.

And Other Stories gratefully acknowledge that our work is
supported using public funding by Arts Council England.

CONTENTS

Nearly six years ago, when I had written the last of my poems for the collection *Green Shadows and Other Poems*, I felt sure that I could write nothing more for publication. I went on writing, of course, but only for my archives.

In mid-2020, during a so-called lockdown in the state of Victoria, I wrote the first few of the pieces in this book — but only for myself and for future readers of my archives. Not until I had mentioned my project to Ivor Indyk of Giramondo, did I think of my pieces as the first of a published collection. Thus encouraged, I went on writing long after the lockdown had ended, pleased to be able yet again to explain myself.

GERALD MURNANE
August 2021

TAMARISK ROW

A few weeks ago, on one of the first days of spring in my eighty-second year, I began a project that seemed likely to provide a neat rounding-off to my career as a published writer. I began to read *Tamarisk Row* (1974), my first book of fiction. I intended to read the book at my leisure and afterwards, in order of their publication, every book of mine, ending with *Green Shadows and Other Poems* (2019). I intended also to write a brief report of my experience as a re-reader of each book. A copy of each report would be lodged in each of my Chronological Archive, which I think of as a documentation of my life as a whole, and my Literary Archive, which is concerned with everything that I've written for publication.

The whole project, before I began it, seemed likely to be reassuring and far from demanding. I looked forward especially to learning about the earlier writer things that he may not have known at the time or things that had since been forgotten. I feel nowadays as though I know immensely more about the writing of fiction than I knew in earlier decades. How would the man I am now judge the earlier man? These and other matters brought on a pleasant sense of anticipation in the days before I began my project.

I had previously read none of my books in its published form. I had looked into each book many times, often for the purpose of finding and then reading – sometimes aloud – one or another passage that I was proud of. I had read aloud more than a few of my favourite passages in public – the last words I had uttered in public comprised the sonorous last paragraph of *A History of Books*. But I had never sat down and tried to confront any book of mine as though for the first time. The word *tried* is the operative word in the previous sentence. I surely knew, when I opened *Tamarisk Row* the other day, that to *try* was as much as I could do.

I discovered early in life that the act of reading is much more complicated than most people seem to acknowledge. My project, as I called it, was never going to be any sort of simple confrontation. And so, while I scanned in their printed form a hundred thousand of the million and more words that I had scrawled in ballpoint pen half a century ago, I did what I've always preferred to do in the presence of a certain sort of text: I followed the workings of my mind.

If I chose to use a common expression, I could report that my mind wandered often from the time when I re-read the first page of *Tamarisk Row*. The word *mind* denotes for me, however, other than it seems to denote for most people, and while I can readily report that some or another conscious part of me was wandering, I would reserve the word *mind* to denote the place where the wandering occurred. I can be much more specific. I can report that for as long as I attended to the text of *Tamarisk Row*, I was distracted by, and sometimes even lost in, the true subject-matter, as I would call it, of that text.

Certain matters mentioned or hinted at in the previous paragraph will be raised again in later sections of this book. I report here only that I had in mind while I read the first, brief section of *Tamarisk Row* far more than the words of that section could have been intended to denote. This should not have surprised me. I had said several times in public that I was for ever prevented from reading any of my published books because I saw their published texts always as surrounded, so to speak, by so much else that had gone into the making of those texts. From among the teeming, infinite-seeming profusion of what I saw, I might mention an image of part of the city of Bendigo as it appeared on a hot afternoon in 1946 to a small boy climbing with his classmates the flights of wooden stairs at the rear of the Capitol Theatre at the upper end of View Street. I might mention a host of persons and places that I recall from the four years that I spent in Bendigo or a host of events that I took part in, although none of those persons or places or events had any bearing on what I wrote about in *Tamarisk Row*. Or I might mention some of the thirty or forty thousand words that I removed from the original text of the work to reduce it to a publishable length, and some of what I saw in mind or felt while I first wrote those words. But the author of a text is not alone in seeing far beyond the simplest denotations and connotations of that text. Surely any self-aware reader knows what a multitude of imagery appears during the reading of a text, often distracting but sometimes enhancing.

In short, I will always have to struggle indeed to decide how any book of mine might affect a reader. But no such struggle need hinder me from assessing the soundness of the sentences that make up the text or the skill and consistency of the narrative. I've learned a great deal about sentences and about narration since I began to write what turned at last into *Tamarisk Row*, and although I could never think of disowning the man who spent his late twenties and early thirties writing his first work of fiction, I expected my re-reading to tell me that my first book was flawed. I knew the sentences would not disappoint me – I've been concerned since boyhood with the structure of sentences – but I expected to find faults in the narration. I had never forgotten the stinging comment by an Irish reviewer that I had grafted an adult's perceptions onto the sensibility of a child.

Needless to say, I found passages that I could wish today to have written differently, but I was more often pleasantly surprised. The author of fifty years ago had thought far less about theories of narration than I have today, but some sort of feeling for the rightness of the narrative was already with him. Throughout my reading, I had in mind the accusation by the Irish reviewer. Had the boy Clement Killeaton been credited with insights beyond his grasp? I had the accusation especially in mind while I read such sections as those reporting Clement's peering of an afternoon into the orange-gold glass panel of the west-facing front door at 42 Leslie Street, Bassett, and I felt wholly exonerated from the Irishman's charge. Twenty and more years before I succeeded in defining for my own satisfaction what I now call 'true fiction' or 'considered narration', I had written page after unerring page of the stuff.

I've spent countless hours during the past sixty years trying to write fiction, but I've also spent a great many hours trying to explain for my own satisfaction *what I'm actually doing* when I'm writing fiction and why I find certain sorts of fiction more satisfying than other sorts. I had been busy at both of those tasks for nearly twenty years before I found the words that I had sought for so long. In fact, I found two neatly complementary sets of words. One set I devised myself. In 1979, I was writing part of the script for a documentary film about myself and my books and my interest in horse-racing. The words I was writing were to come from my own mouth while I was standing alone before the camera. I had come to dislike and distrust cameras by then, and I was perhaps provoked to declare to the darkness behind the lens what I had previously been unable to write on a blank page. Or, perhaps I supposed my situation was that of the narrator of the last passage of *The Plains*, and the camera in front of me was aimed only at the darkness behind my eyes. Whatever, as they say, in the film *Words and Silk* I declare at length what I can state simply here: true fiction is an account of certain of the contents of the mind of the narrator.

The second of the two sets of words I found in the introduction to a paperback collection of the short works of Herman Melville. Given the importance of those words to me and the number of times I've quoted or paraphrased them, it might be expected that I could name the author of the words, but I can't. His name would be somewhere among my lecture notes in my Chronological Archive, but the notes amount to several hundred pages, and the book where I first read the words is in storage in Melbourne, four hundred kilometres away. So, the author, who was a male and a lesser-known academic, if dead by now never knew or if still alive will never know that a few of his words had a life-changing impact on one of his fellows. Those words are to the effect that a story well told informs us not only that certain things may have happened but *what it is to know that such things may have happened.*

It would not be inapt for me to mention here my having described myself sometimes as a technical writer: one whose fiction is no more and no less than an accurate report of some of the contents of his mind. For this sort of writer – my sort of writer – a passage of fiction is not an account of something that might once have happened in the visible world; it is not even an account of something that could conceivably have happened in that world. For this sort of writer, such issues are irrelevant; a passage of fiction reports his or her *contemplation* of what did happen or what did not happen or what might have happened or what can never happen.

While I read recently many a passage from *Tamarisk Row*, I enjoyed many a seeming-memory, as I would call it, of myself in my early thirties in what my wife and I called the book-room (before it became our eldest son's bedroom) during the several hundreds of evenings and weekends when I wrote the last drafts of what is called, on the rear cover of the 2008 edition, my masterpiece. I enjoyed, for example, the seeming-memory of myself writing not what I myself saw when I looked sometimes of an afternoon through the translucent yellowish glass in the front door of a weatherboard cottage at 244 Neale Street, Bendigo, thirty and more years before, and not what some readily visible character saw in some readily visible film-in-the-mind, but what came to light, to use that impressive figure of speech, when, in a certain north-facing room in a certain north-eastern suburb of Melbourne, I wrote that a certain fictional personage stood before a pane of sunlit glass and when I got ready to report the patterns of imagery already rising to sight in the endless, inexhaustible place-of-places that I demean when I call it my mind.

While I was writing the previous sentence, I was reassured yet again of the truth of the claim by the narrator of my 'First Love' (first published in the collection *Velvet Waters*, 1990), that no such thing as 'Time' exists; that we experience only place after place; that remembering, as we call it, is no sort of rediscovery or recollection but an act performed for the very first time somewhere in the endless place known as the present.

By way of illustrating my preferred form of narration, I could cite the section of *Tamarisk Row* titled 'The field lines up for the Gold Cup race'. That section is one of a number of passages in the book that can surely not be taken to represent the thoughts or the imaginings of any character. Nor am I willing to agree that the passage is any sort of commentary or intervention by a narrator such as Thomas Hardy or Anthony Trollope employed. I prefer to leave unnamed the source of the passage and not to connect it closely to any one character. Of course I wrote the passage, and of course, by a crude process of elimination, it must be attributed to the narrator, but during the complex process of the reading of true fiction, such exactitude is not called for. If, during that mysterious process, a reader can mistake a character for himself or herself, then the same reader can likewise err with the narrator or the narrator err with either of the other two.

I seem to recall several critics pointing out that my first published work contained many, if not most, of the themes or strands to be found in my later works. I found plenty of evidence for this during my re-reading. I should have been annoyed, perhaps, by my wastefulness – using in an overly long first work what should have been husbanded for the future. Or, I should have been a bit ashamed of my nervousness as an unpublished writer – putting on display far more than was needed to impress a likely publisher. Instead, I learned that I myself, in the person of the narrator of my first work of fiction, had foreseen the inevitable. To quote the course broadcaster towards the end of his call of the Gold Cup race: '... he knows at last that he will never leave Tamarisk Row ...'

A SEASON ON EARTH

I have my own way of assessing the worth of a book – not just a so-called work of literature but any sort of book or, for that matter, any piece of music or any so-called work of art. I could say in simple terms that I judge the worth of a book according to the length of time during which the book stays in my mind, but I can't pass up the opportunity to explain how the reading of a book or the remembering of a book are not for me what they seem to be for many others.

James Joyce, so I once read, was often irritated by someone's reporting that he or she had just read a most impressive book. The person so impressed would begin to explain the impressive subject-matter of the book, but Joyce could not tolerate this. He wanted to learn what the book truly comprised; he wanted the enthused reader to quote from the text of the book some of the more impressive sentences or paragraphs. This, of course, few enthused readers are able to do. I myself am seldom able to do it, but at least I learned long ago not to claim that I was talking about a *book* when what I was talking about were my memories or my impressions or my fantasies.

Sometimes an impressive sentence or two will stay with me for long afterwards. I have not looked into *Moby-Dick*, by Herman Melville, for fifty-three years, but I can recall a sentence that still comes to me sometimes and works its strange effect on me: a simple sentence spoken by Captain Ahab not long before the final pursuit of the white whale. 'They are making hay in the meadows of the Andes, Mr Starbuck.' And if someone should ever inform me that those are not the exact words of the text, I'll be pleased rather than abashed – pleased that I've adapted a fictional text for the best of all purposes: to enrich an actual life.

My own books, those that I wrote, have always seemed, of course, far more than mere texts. The actual published words seem to me sometimes mere traces of long-lasting moods, oppressed states of mind, or whole phases of my life, but some of those published words sometimes appear in written form or sound aloud in my mind, or sometimes I call on them for encouragement or consolation. The examples that I'm about to quote occurred to me while I was writing just now about the sentence from *Moby-Dick*, and I may well have composed my often remembered sentence under the influence of the strange mood brought on by Melville's sentence. My sentence is part of a passage towards the end of *Inland* in which passage the narrator ponders on the frequent occurrence in works of literature or music of a calm or serene passage before the major themes engage in their final, climactic conflict: *The solemn themes turn to face the storm.*

Given that I recall nothing from so many of the books that I've read, *Moby-Dick* rates highly with me, and if I were to learn from one reader alone that one sentence alone from the text of *Inland* still recurred to him or her, then I would hope that my book would rate equally highly with that reader.

My preferred words for my most esteemed books are *memorable* and *influential*, and those words certainly describe *Hunger*, by Knut Hamsun. Nothing of the text remains with me from my having read it about forty years ago. What remain are either memories of mental scenery brought into being while I read or, more likely, re-creations of such scenery prompted by powerful feelings liable to be aroused by the mere calling to mind of the title of the book and the name of its author. Under the influence of those feelings several years ago, and at a time when I often claimed I had nothing further to write, I spent several days making notes for a book-length work of fiction titled *Thirst* that might affect at least one reader as Knut Hamsun's book had affected me. I was tired of writing for publication, but the desire to emulate Hamsun might have kept me going if I had not come to understand, while I made my notes, that I had already written during my fourth decade, and before I had read *Hunger*, a book such as I felt driven to write in my ninth.

Readers never tire of asking me how closely the lives of my fictional characters and narrators resemble my own life, and I persist in giving evasive answers. The two most common are hardly dishonest. I declare that separating accurate memories from their various counterparts is a hard task. Or, I declare that my own life in Bendigo during the 1940s or in Oakleigh South in the 1950s was much stranger than Clement Killeaton's life in Bassett or Adrian Sherd's in Accrington. Here, however, is a freely given morsel for my persistent questioners to seize on.

In the third section of *A Season on Earth*, Adrian is a student of a seminary conducted by a religious order of

Catholic priests. The year is 1955. Many of my readers will know that I was a seminarian for a time. (Some accounts seem to suggest that I studied for the priesthood for several years. In fact, I spent fourteen weeks in the seminary in early 1957.) Adrian's motives may be interpreted from the text of *A Season on Earth* and also from the variant passages in the last pages of the first section of *A Lifetime on Clouds*. My own motives for applying to join the Congregation of the Passion (Passionist Fathers) were different indeed from Adrian's.

Regardless of what I may have said to myself or to others at the time, I surely knew that I turned to the priesthood in order to avoid going to university. And if I didn't admit my true motive then for fear that it proved me a social and emotional retard, I proudly admit it now and declare that my decision was in my own best interests. I was dux of my class all through secondary school and winner each year of the prize for English Literature. Reading was hugely important to me, and I was already trying to write poetry. Even so, I found the *study* of English distasteful, hateful even, and wholly confusing. And although I knew hardly anything of what went on in universities, I sensed that the study of English there would be even less to my liking. Perhaps I sensed that I would one day define for my own satisfaction why the reading of a certain sort of book seemed necessary for my peace of mind, if not for my very survival. Certainly I knew that what I wrote in essays had little connection with the all-important question why certain texts had a profound and lasting effect on me while others had none.

I claimed earlier that *A Season on Earth* is somehow similar to *Hunger*. I would have been more precise if I had written that I consider Adrian Sherd and the first-person narrator of *Hunger* to be similar personages and their predicaments somewhat similar. Each personage strides by day or broods and scribbles by night in his native city, but as though an invisible pane separates him from its other inhabitants and an invisible grip prevents him from living as they live. Adrian, for example, feels especially deprived in his never having seen a naked female or even an illustration of one such. He decides that his most practical means for remedying this is to save his money and eventually to travel to Yemen where, so he has read, young women may be bought as slaves and inspected by the buyers beforehand. In the last of the four sections of the book, Adrian moves rapidly through one after another of the four dream-roles that he had earlier played out for a year and more each: satyr, loving husband, priest, and poet. But his moving thus is no sort of resolution. The invisible pane still bars his way; the invisible grip still holds him back. The women he lusts after or falls in love with are depictions in newspapers or magazines. The monastery that he wants to join is in England. His literary projects are mere daydreams. I cannot agree with those readers who believe that Adrian, as he appears in the last pages of the book, is ready to become any sort of competent writer.

I once went to much trouble to buy a collection of the writings of Karl Kraus. I found them unreadable, and yet I've always been grateful to Kraus for admitting boldly to a failing that I thought peculiarly mine: for admitting that he did not understand what philosophers do. I understand what philosophers *try* to do, which is what most of us surely spend our lives trying to do, but I do not understand their reports of their efforts. I could say the same about most literary critics and book reviewers, with the difference that I'm willing to compete with them in their field.

I said in the fourth paragraph of this section that my own books seem more than texts but they are, of course, mere texts: words arranged in sentences. What I find endlessly interesting is our agreeing to write and to talk about the entities denoted by those words as though the entities are no less substantial than the persons who write and talk about them. I myself made use of this agreement just now when I was writing about Adrian Sherd. I made use of a common convention but I would prefer never to have to do so. I would prefer to speak and to write always factually about fictional texts and about the imagery that exists only in my own mind when I read such texts or when I remember having read them.

Some readers have had with Adrian Sherd the trouble that some reviewers and commentators have when they confuse mental and actual events. A colleague of mine in a tertiary institute once told me that many in her Literature class supposed that Adrian actually talks with Denise and engages with her in the last pages of the second section of the book. And yes, my choice of words in the previous sentence demonstrates the near-impossibility of writing or speaking with exactitude about the workings of fiction. It may demonstrate also my inability to cope with philosophy.

In 1957, after I had returned from my brief stay in the seminary, I was free of course to begin an Arts degree in the following year. I was certainly well qualified, having obtained honours in every subject in the matriculation exam in the previous year. (I earned first class honours in English

Literature by writing what I supposed I was expected to write and certainly not what I thought and felt about the set texts. I wonder sometimes what inanities I wrote about *Wuthering Heights*, a book that has stayed with me throughout the six and more decades since my matriculation studies.) Instead, I enrolled at a primary teachers' college and completed a two-year course that qualified me to teach in primary schools. I had no ambition to be more than a primary teacher of average achievement, but in my free time I was going to strive to become a published poet.

My teacher-training course would take me no further than the middle ranks, and in 1964 I overcame my distaste for university studies and enrolled as an evening student in English One at the University of Melbourne. I had no wish to shine and I expected to learn nothing that would help me as a writer. A lowly pass was all I needed to improve my standing as an employee of the Education Department of Victoria. I soon found that even so little was going to be hard to achieve.

I was no trouble-maker or rebel. I wanted only to learn what was the orthodox view of each set text and then to paraphrase that view in my essays and exam answers. I soon learned, however, that most of the staff of the English Department were followers of F. R. Leavis and were unwilling or unable to allow that anyone could respond to a literary text other than as a Leavisite. Why did I not read some of Leavis's creed and adopt it as my own for the time being? I would have just done that if I could have understood the Great Man's creed. What little I understood repelled me; the rest made no sense.

In my Chronological Archive, as I call it, is an essay that I wrote as a student of English during the era when Leavis ruled. The essay earned me eleven marks out of twenty – a bare pass. One of the many harsh comments written in the margins by my tutor accused me of 'radical confusion to do with the way morality shows itself in a work of art'. Half a century later, I wrote on the carefully preserved handwritten essay the following reply to the tutor's comment: 'You were right, and I was even confused as to what *is* morality and what *is* art. I am none the wiser today, but my radical confusion has never caused me the least distress.'

What *has* sometimes caused me distress is to think of the many hours that I, and others like me, wasted as students of English on a pointless and probably impossible task. The same tutor who so accurately diagnosed my radical confusion once paused in class after she had used the word 'tone', which was one of Leavis's favourites. 'You should be acquiring by now a critical vocabulary,' she told us, 'and the word *tone* should be an essential item in it.'

So! Even if we couldn't understand the content of our course, we knew now the aim of it. We were to be turned into literary critics. We were to become adept at asserting how 'one' or 'we' respond to texts. We were to approve or disapprove of them according to principles finally discovered, and promulgated once and for all, by a narrow-minded and truculent splitter of hairs in Cambridge.

Who were *we*? I'm referring not to the dispassionate, discriminating, hypothetical personages whose responses to texts were charted by the Leavisites in their critical essays, but to the student body in the evening classes for English

One that I attended in the early 1960s. We were mostly in our early or mid-twenties; many of us were fully employed by day; and many of the employed were primary teachers needing a degree, or even a few subjects, for promotion to higher ranks. We teachers had charge, by day, of classes of forty and more primary-school children in distant suburbs. We dismissed our classes promptly at three-thirty on the day of our weekly English lectures and tutorials and hurried, mostly by train or tram or bus, towards the distant university. Some of us had a snack on the way; the rest sat through the evening class with empty stomachs. Few of us reached home before eight and all of us, of course, had to get up as usual next morning to teach our classes. We endured these moderate hardships, as I've said, for the sake of our careers as teachers, and many of us had no other motive. We took notes during lectures and listened closely during tutorials only so that we could learn what we were expected to write in essays and exam papers. All we wanted was to get a degree and to go back to real life, as we would have called it.

A few of us however – who knows how very few? – wanted much more than this. We had learned as children that the things happening to us while we read a certain sort of book had more power over us than most of the things happening around us in the world where we sat and read. We had learned that some of the personages who appeared to us while we read seemed closer to us than most of the persons in the world where we sat and read. We had learned that we were apt to fall in love with those personages at least as readily as we fell in love with those persons. We had learned these things and much else while we read, and we hoped that the study of English at university might help us understand these things.

While I was writing the previous paragraph, I remembered a statement made by a professor of English at a time when some or another work of fiction had been banned from being imported into Australia from the USA on the grounds that parts of it were obscene. The professor was not from the University of Melbourne and was surely not a Leavisite. He referred first to a small collection of books in the library at his university: a collection dealing with sexual pathology. The only persons allowed access to the collection were students of psychiatric medicine, presumably on the grounds that those persons were embarked on a study of the human personality in its farthest reaches. Well, argued the professor of English, students of *his* discipline were, in their own way, embarked on the same study. Why were his students prevented from reading the banned book, which had been set for their course?

I finally scraped through a major in English as part of my bachelor's degree, hating every aspect of the course. During each of my summer holidays as a part-time student, I tried to go on with the latest draft of *Tamarisk Row*. I never felt that the sort of writing I had done in my essays and exam papers was in any way connected with my fiction-writing.

Certain passages in the last of the four sections of *A Season on Earth* report Adrian as trying to regulate as much as possible of his daily life so that it demonstrates the influence on him of his latest literary hero. Adrian dresses, for example, as he supposes A. E. Housman dressed. Adrian even tries to stride as his poet-hero might have strode. Some readers have seen this as evidence that Adrian is preparing to be himself an author. Other readers might see it as evidence that Adrian is unhinged. For the purposes of this piece of writing, I want to assert that Adrian knows more about English literature than did any of my teachers at university. And I would much rather learn from Adrian Maurice Sherd how to engage with certain literary texts than from Frank Raymond Leavis.

THE PLAINS

Perhaps twenty years ago, I was introduced to a young Englishwoman who had just been appointed some sort of agent for the Australian publisher of *The Plains* (not the original publisher, who had gone out of business, as the publishers of unclassifiable books tend to do). She had been told a great deal about my best-known book, so the young woman said, and she was dying to read it, but she was saving the experience until her journey homewards – she wanted to read *The Plains* while she was flying over the vast red centre of Australia. I said nothing – just hoped she wouldn't be overly disappointed.

My first two books were published only two years apart, but nothing further of mine appeared for six years until *The Plains* was published by Norstrilia Press in 1982. I've experienced good times and bad during my career, but those six years were the hardest to bear. Quite apart from some problems in my private life, I wasted a year and more trying to rewrite the still-unpublished later sections of *A Season on Earth* into a self-contained work: a sort of sequel to *A Lifetime on Clouds*. When that proved impossible, I wrote, with much trouble, a book-length work of fiction titled *The Only Adam*, which was then rejected for publication by two publishers.

Or, was it *three*? I prefer not to consult my records of those miserable years.

I had paid a friend of mine to type the text of the rejected work. He happened at the time to be setting up a small firm to publish what he and his co-founders called speculative fiction. After *The Only Adam* had failed to find a publisher, my friend made me an offer. What is now known as the text of *The Plains*, together with a few hundred words as yet unpublished, comprised four separate sections interleaved with the four sections of *The Only Adam*. The offer was to publish as a book in its own right the first three of the four interleaved sections, the setting of which was a landscape of plains. Having been unpublished for five years, and with no project underway, I gladly accepted the offer. Matters went smoothly after that, except for a disagreement over the title. I wanted the book to be called *Landscape with Darkness and Mirage*. The publishers wanted *The Plains*, and I eventually gave way, which is something I still sometimes regret. My best-known book is the only one of all my books with the definite article as the first word of its title.

Since my early years as a writer, I've been turned against works of fiction with titles such as 'The Haunting' or 'The Affair', which seem to me mere labels stuck on by authors unable to recognise the underlying patterns of meaning in their work or unable, probably, to conceive of such patterns. The best of my titles are meant to add to the meaning of a work or to draw the reader's attention to a strand of meaning not obvious at first approach.

The Englishwoman, of course, was free to connect my book with the Outback, although she was surely going to find nothing in the text to support her when she got around to reading it. Soon after the publication of the book, the dim-witted literary editor of a Melbourne newspaper told me he was baffled by the reference in the early pages to a hotel of at least three storeys. He knew of no town in rural Victoria with a hotel of that size, so he said, and he wanted to know where exactly *The Plains* was meant to be set. I guessed that he had not read past the opening pages, but he was the first literary editor who had deigned to interview me, and so I told him politely that the book was not *set* anywhere, as he understood the word, but my telling him this seemed only to add to his confusion.

And yet, everything I write is set somewhere. No matter what I'm writing, some sort of imagery is present to my mind's eye, as it used to be called. Besides, I've often claimed to be incapable of abstract thought and to think of my mind itself as a place with infinite-seeming landscapes, all of which suggests that even when I was reporting the most complex details of the cultural heritage of the Plainsmen, I was aware that the harsh light at the edges of the drawn blinds (much of the action, so to call it, takes place indoors) resembled a sort of light that I had seen at some time in the visible world.

I had certainly not seen that light in the Outback. In January 1964, I travelled to Streaky Bay in South Australia by way of Port Augusta, which probably entitles me to say that I've glimpsed the edges of the Outback, but what I saw made no impression. The plains that I'm trying to locate were more a presence than a perceptible landscape. They are the presence that I divined on January afternoons in Bendigo in the mid-1940s, when I stayed indoors and played with my glass marbles on the mat and when the north wind rattled the window-panes and sent tremors through the brownish holland blinds. They could equally well be the presence that I likewise divined on warm days in the spring of 1949, during the few months when we lived in what had been the home of my father's parents on the coast east of Warrnambool. The plains north of Bendigo I had never seen (and have still never seen), but the plains north-east of Warrnambool I had several times crossed, glimpsing sometimes the far-off bluestone mansion of some notable pastoral family.

Yes, this or that image of plains helped in the writing of my best-known book, but what I chiefly stared at when the words were slow in arriving was a common shrub: a cotoneaster bush beside a fence of drab palings bordering a backyard in a suburb of Melbourne.

For much of my writing life, I had no room of my own and not even a desk to sit at. If the house was quiet or if my wife and sons were absent, I preferred to write on a bar-stool at the kitchen bench. If this was not possible, I took the ironing-board into my wife's and my bedroom and shut the door behind me and used the cloth-covered, unstable ironing-board as my desk, with only a blank expanse of wall ahead if I looked up from my typewriter. But whenever I recall the actual writing of the text now known as *The Plains*, or the periods of idleness between the bouts of actual writing, I recall chiefly the unremarkable view through the kitchen window from my seat beside the bench.

The act of writing, or even merely the attempt to write, has brought to me countless times what I'll call for present purposes *revelations*. The most valuable of these unsought

31

bonuses arrive about a half-hour after the actual writing or effort to write. I wrote my sentence about the cotoneaster bush at the end of an afternoon of writing, and when I put away my pages I supposed the only comment I might write next day was on the seeming unconnectedness, on those mornings in the winter of 1978, between what I looked at and what I wrote about. But less than an hour later I was made aware, all at once, of the meaning for me of the most wayward of my books.

The Plains has been explained and interpreted in numerous ways, and this I consider a tribute to the richness and the complexity of a work of fiction having, as someone once commented, hardly any plot or characters. I'm pleased also that *The Plains* is a book I can point to when the claim is made that my fiction too much resembles fictionalised autobiography. But the question that most engages me with every book of mine is not 'What does it mean?' but 'Why did I write it?' or, more specifically, 'What pattern of meaning has it revealed in my mind?' The answer has almost always come to me during the writing of the book in question, but until a few days ago I had been for nearly forty years less than satisfied with the various seeming-explanations for the existence of my best-known book.

Plants interest me only if I associate them with events in my actual history or my mental history, and I've never had any reason to be interested in the cotoneaster, with its dull-green leaves, insignificant blooms, and the red berries that form an unpleasant mush underfoot. Why then did this backyard bush continually overhang, as it were, the dazzling enormity of the Plains? (And surely they deserve that upper-case letter.) Well, the common red berries of the cotoneaster have sometimes, to put the matter simply, reminded me of a plant that was familiar to me for a few years during my childhood although I've seldom seen it since and have never learned its name. The plant was a garden shrub with orange-coloured berries, and I'm writing now about a specimen that stood in the spacious garden surrounding a house that I visualised throughout my childhood whenever I read or heard the words *luxurious* or *palatial*.

In an early section of *Tamarisk Row* is a brief account of Clement's meeting up with two older girls in the garden surrounding the home of Stan Riordan the bookmaker. The girls are playing a guessing game with coloured berries called, for the purposes of the game, eggs in the bush. Clement persuades the girls to let him join them in the game but they later expel him because he cannot grasp the rules.

After having written the previous paragraph, I looked at the actual text of my first book. According to the text, the girls *invite* Clement to join them. If I had not consulted the text, I would have gone on to write in *this* text several statements at odds with the published account of the game played with berries. Something else happened now to confuse matters further. When I tried to recall from my own childhood the actual incident that was later embellished in a work of fiction and later still misremembered, I was unable to call up the details.

What I've just reported is surely a common occurrence for many writers of fiction. What is surely uncommon is for a core or a knot of fictional imagery, long since severed from its roots in actuality, to reveal itself after an interval

33

of forty or more years as the encrypted key to the meaning of a whole work of fiction in which the core or knot itself is never mentioned. For this is precisely what has happened while I've re-read *The Plains* and reported on my experience. Nothing so crude could have happened as that the sight of the cotoneaster berries somehow directed me in my writing of *The Plains*. The process that led me to write that book had for long been in place before I first sat at the kitchen bench and stared at the windows above the sink. No, something much more remarkable happened. While I was writing what became *The Plains*, I would have been aware of a host of details from my surroundings and my daily routine, but whenever during the subsequent forty years I've wanted to recall the circumstances of my writing that book, the memory that recurs and recurs is of the shrub with the red berries.

The Plains is by far the best known of my books, to judge from the number of foreign editions and from the attention given to it by scholars. Even local critics who paid scant attention to my first two books accorded me a new level of respect after the appearance of my slender third book with its drab dust-jacket and the imprint of a little-known publisher. Few of the book's many admirers can have had any notion of its unlikely origins as a sort of florid descant accompanying a conventional narrative. The earliest draft was in the third person and had, instead of a nameless first-person narrator, a chief character designated only by an upper-case A. (The chief character of what I've called the conventional narrative had a surname beginning with the same letter.)

I would have to search among my earliest notes and drafts in order to learn what I thought I was doing when I began to write what later became *The Plains*, but even that might tell me no more than would my present-day conjectures, given that I've learned a good deal about my ways as a writer during the past forty years. When I think now of the man who sat at the kitchen bench and who stared at the cotoneaster shrub, which I see now as dripping with rain, and when I think of the boy in the grounds of the palatial-seeming house thirty years earlier again, struggling to learn the baffling rules of the game with the coloured berries, I'm prompted to add my own eccentric interpretation to the many put forward by critics and commentators.

The unnamed narrator of *The Plains* may seem to some readers a sort of explorer or researcher or even a would-be film-maker. Most of what he reports of his twenty years of note-taking and his absorption in cultural niceties – most of this seems to me, however, the most elaborate and protracted of courtship rituals. If I know anything about him, he is searching first for his ideal landscape and then for the female person or personage at the heart of that elusive hinterland. The girls and the women that he observes from afar and plans to approach by devious means are somewhat to him what the older girls in the bookmaker's garden are to Clement Killeaton. Their conduct is governed by rules that he struggles to grasp. He must find a way of proving himself worthy to join them.

I wonder whether some of the previous few paragraphs may have disappointed or even annoyed a certain sort of reader. Of all the praise directed at my third book, one claim in particular has stayed with me during the four decades since I first read it in an early review. In *The Plains*, according to the reviewer, *the mind of Australia* is delineated. (This assertion, I have to admit, baffles me almost as much as it gratifies me.) If a writer could be credited with having an understanding of the mind of a nation, should not that writer be supposed to have arrived at that understanding after rigorous research and the sort of thinking attributed to philosophers? Conversely, is any significant intellectual achievement likely to result from a struggling writer's staring at an unkempt backyard and reporting the failed endeavours and the personal inadequacies of a fictional personage, all the while unaware that his, the writer's, yearning and despair may be what drives him to write?

In my Chronological Archive is a folder labelled *Csodák – Miracles.* The folder contains nearly fifty thousand words reporting nearly fifty experiences of mine that seem to me miraculous according to a definition of my own devising. None of those experiences is in any way connected with my authorship of *The Plains*, but when I've finished this essay I should, perhaps, make good that omission. It seems no less than miraculous that the text of *The Plains* might well have been created as I've just now surmised: that the primitive rudiments of the text might well have been formed on an afternoon of fierce sunlight in the 1940s, when a child who is by now as much a fictional personage as an actual boy stood a little apart from two self-assured young female persons among vistas of lawns and shrubbery beside a splendid house in the grandest city of the goldfields of Victoria and when he first divined the vastness of what he was by birth entitled to dream of and the narrowness of what he was by nature likely to obtain.

And what about *The Only Adam*? Couldn't it be fetched from my Literary Archive and published with sections of

The Plains inserted in it as once they were? Left to myself, I could never have decided what to do in this matter, but a few years ago I was persuaded by one of my two separate publishers to let them read the long-buried typescript and to consider its possible publication. To judge from the length of time they took, the publisher and his advisers were no more sure than I am today about *The Only Adam*. I had told them I'd agree with whatever they decided, and in the end they decided against publication. The situation will be different after my death. My Literary Archive, together with my two other archives, will be sold by my executors to some or another Australian library. In due course, anyone will be free to inspect the archives, and the executors will be free to publish any part of them.

I can only guess how the original text of *The Only Adam* will seem to the same scholars who have found so much meaning in the sections now known collectively as *The Plains*. No sort of mock-modesty prevents me from calling *The Plains* an extraordinary work of fiction. No sort of pride or vanity prevents me from calling the rest of *The Only Adam* rather ordinary. I wrote it during the lowest period of my writing career, when I seemed unlikely to have any further work of mine published. The few people to have read the whole of *The Only Adam* have each commented on the great difference between the sections that became *The Plains* and the other sections. I explain that difference by declaring that one part of the work was written for the purest of all motives – it was written because it *had* to be written. The other part was written for a base motive – it was written to meet the expectations of a conjectured publisher.

LANDSCAPE WITH
LANDSCAPE

I can't begin to imagine what may have been discovered about the workings of the human brain during the fifty and more years since I decided that my brain cells were none of my business. Until I decided thus, in my twenty-sixth year, I had felt an obligation to keep myself well informed about all sorts of matters. When I decided thus, I was reading an article for the general reader about the work of the American neurosurgeon Wilder Penfield. The article ended as most similar articles end, with the journalist-author using such phrases as 'imminent discoveries' and 'unlocking the secrets'.

While I read, I felt none of the eager anticipation that the writer of the article felt or affected to feel. I had had nothing of note published at the time, but I considered my life's work to be writing, by which I meant writing poetry or fiction, and despite my having achieved so little, I felt an underlying confidence and even envisaged myself sometimes as making imminent discoveries of my own or unlocking my own sorts of secret. But these dreamed-of activities would not take place in the visible world: the world of matter. I could hardly have found at that time the words to explain myself, but I knew that my tasks as a writer would involve me with moods, feelings, mental imagery, and with doubts, confusion, and imprecision, and whether or not these vague entities depended for their existence on electrical impulses or brain cells was of no interest to me.

Anything that I write about my mind grossly over-simplifies it. I often declare that I think of my mind as a place, but no place in this, the visible world, could be half so resistant to exploration as even the most familiar of mental landscapes. And if my sort of writing is a sort of mapping of mind, then my atlas should depict nothing more stable than images and feelings.

The Plains has had more attention than any other of my books, but I consider my best-known book no more worthy of attention than the book that followed it: *Landscape with Landscape*. And because that book still seems to me unjustly neglected, I'll make the provocative claim that 'The Battle of Acosta Nu', the third of the six separate components of the book, seems to its author hardly less deserving of attention than *The Plains*.

While I re-read 'The Battle of Acosta Nu', I reflected on the complexity behind the writing of it. I learned the truth of the claim by some writers that the worthiest of subject-matter is not chosen by its seeming-author but assembles itself in a place of its own and then forces itself through the author and onto the page.

In February 1977, one of my sons was taken by his mother, my wife, to the Royal Children's Hospital in Melbourne feverish and semi-conscious. He was found to be badly infected with the bacterium known as golden staph. He was dosed with a proven medicine, but my wife told me when I arrived later at the hospital that the boy's specialist physician had warned that he might well die. The account of the illness and death of the narrator's son in 'The Battle of Acosta Nu' is fiction, of course, but all the medical details in the fiction can be read as an accurate report of what happened to my son — all the details except one. The doctor who came to me from the intensive care unit did indeed have shoes that squeaked, but what he told me was that he and his colleague had got my son's heart beating again and that the boy was attached to a respirator and no longer in danger.

The fictional narrative comes to an end not long after the doctor's announcement, but my son spent six weeks in hospital recovering from his ordeal. I had ample time to spend at his bedside. I was a house-husband at the time, caring for my other two sons and supported by a one-year fellowship from the Australia Council. I had done no writing since my son had fallen ill, and even if the time had been available I could never have brought myself to write a word of fiction until he had fully recovered. Some writers would surely have found relief by dashing off at such a time a factual or even fictional account of recent events, but my sort of fiction cannot be thus written, as these very pages are meant to explain. The young registrar of the ward was tireless and conscientious, but I could never forget that he had failed to foresee the developments that had almost killed my son on the fateful night. I dealt with the man politely, and he may have been trying to ease the situation between us when he said to me one day that he had heard I was a writer and that he supposed I would one day put into a novel some of what my family and I had recently undergone. I soon forgot whatever I replied, but I was by then not only a writer but a student of all matters to do with the writing of fiction and although I never doubted I would one day write about the recent ordeal, I had no way of knowing when I would thus write or in what context.

I first read about the Australians in Paraguay in a popular illustrated magazine in the late 1950s or early 1960s. An enterprising journalist had found and interviewed some Paraguayan descendants of the original settlers. I longed to know more but I did nothing to ease my longing. I seem to have anticipated even then what I later learned to expect with confidence whenever some or another likely subject-matter had appeared to me: either that providence would bring me, all in good time, whatever I still needed or that the meagre details already available to me would one day reveal their true depth or intensity and would be more than enough for my needs.

In the last months of 1968, my wife was expecting our first child. She and I had lived for nearly three years since our marriage in a third-floor flat in an inner northern suburb of Melbourne. On many a morning since our moving-in, I had looked north-east from the kitchen window of the flat. In the far distance was the dark-blue ridge of the Kinglake Ranges. In the nearer distance were the hilly suburbs of Ivanhoe and Heidelberg. My wife and I were saving to buy a house in some or another suburb between those two prominences and to live out our lives there, and it seemed appropriate that the place we were destined for was just beyond view. On Christmas Day in 1968, the baby's birth was only weeks away and we were soon to move to our new home. The day itself was gloomy, with low cloud and drizzling rain and humid air. I spent most of the day reading from beginning to end a book that had been recently published. I had mentioned the book to my wife and she had given it to me as a present: *A Peculiar People: The Australians in Paraguay*, by Gavin Souter.

My mood for most of that day was so intense and so unusual that I can still recall it, fifty years later. I am not about to report that I thought of relieving or expressing my mood by writing a powerful piece of fiction. No such thought would have occurred to me on Christmas Day 1968, or for some years afterwards. All my spare time and energy in those days went into my struggle to write *Tamarisk Row*, and I've never understood how a writer of fiction could be drawn to write about historical events, so to call them. No, I'm recalling my first encounter with Souter's text as an example of an experience which, of itself, might never have driven me to write, no matter how powerfully it had affected me.

The earlier drafts of 'The Battle of Acosta Nu' are dated 1979. So, about two years after my son's illness I was empowered to write fiction about the meaning for his father of that illness. But how was I thus empowered? That was a rhetorical question, of course. The only person who could even begin to answer it is myself, and I decline the challenge. I decline to speculate about abstractions such as *emotion* or *reason* or *memory*, and as I wrote above, I leave my brain cells to their own devices. All I know is that connections take place between such disparate matters as the near-death of a child in 1977 and the failure of a utopian colony in a far-away country nearly a century earlier; connections take place, and the connecting medium is the stuff of mental imagery and of feelings; connections take place; surfaces give way to depths; entities combine or divide; revelations of all kinds occur in the place that I call, for want of a better term, *my mind* and the benefits that I derive from these processes and from my knowing that these processes take place continually and are taking place even now as I write about them – those benefits are my true reward for writing fiction.

On all but a very few Saturdays during my adult years, I've either attended the Melbourne races or, at least, heard them described on radio. One of those very few was a Saturday in August 1984, when the races were at Sandown and the main race was the weight-for-age Liston Stakes. I had been working intermittently on *Landscape with Landscape* for five years or more, and in order to complete it I had promised the finished typescript to my publisher by a certain date. My ploy worked, but in the last weeks before the deadline I had to give up more and more non-essential tasks, and on the very last Saturday I shut myself away all day and only learned the race results from the Sunday newspaper. That last Saturday was given over to typing the final draft of the last piece in the book, 'Landscape with Artist'. Most of the text seemed complete, but a few passages still needed rewriting. One such passage was a report of the narrator's standing in front of a portrait of a woman and speaking to the painted image. The passage as it stood gave me a peculiar satisfaction, but I felt urged to rewrite the last sentence.

I could walk right now to the fourth of the sixteen crowded filing-cabinet drawers containing my Literary Archive and could learn what was the earlier version of the sentence that I rewrote on Liston Stakes Day thirty-six years ago, but

I prefer simply to recite aloud the perfected sentence. *I hear from myself a voice I have wanted for a long time to hear.*

In the third paragraph before this, I celebrated the richness of meaning to be found in a long passage of fiction or a whole work. I now acknowledge the sentence alone as a unit of meaning. Much of the meaning of the quoted sentence derives from its context, of course, and for the alert, sympathetic reader the sentence should sound with all the aptness of the final bars of a musical composition. But I've been for most of my writing career alert to the sounds and the cadences and the order of the phrases and the clauses in sentences, and I get pleasure from reciting by heart the sentences that impress me. Most of my favourite sentences from my own works are too long to be learned by heart. The quoted sentence is of the right length, except that it needed no learning; it has stayed with me from the day when I first composed it.

An early reviewer of my fourth book described it as a feminist reader's nightmare. I still find her comment astonishing. The reviewer had a doctorate in Australian literature, and I could only suppose that her feminist convictions must have prevented her from recognising what seems to me obvious: that the narrators of all six pieces in *Landscape with Landscape* are at heart scarcely different from the narrator of *The Plains* in that they are awed by women, baffled by them, and in various degrees afraid of them. Once again, I've gone against my own strong convictions by writing about fictional characters as though they are actual persons. I might have done better to write just now about someone who is unquestionably an actual person: the author of *Landscape with Landscape* – and not just the implied author, knowable only by means of the text that he produced, but the flesh-and-blood author or the breathing author, as I like to call him. I wrote the six pieces in my book in an order quite different from their order in the published volume. The last piece to be written was 'Landscape with Freckled Woman', which is, of course, the first in the book as it is now. I wanted the first piece to serve in some ways as an overture serves in an opera. The narrator of the piece is far more obviously a writer than are the other five narrators in the book. He speculates at length about such complex matters as the connections between an actual woman and a fictional woman in a work that he hopes to write. Re-reading my own words a few days ago, I had to absorb them slowly and intently for fear of becoming confused. I recalled another unfavourable review of the book by a fool who supposed that the narrator passed himself off as a writer in order to seduce women. If the final text was no simple narrative, how much more tangled might the early drafts have been?

I went to the archive now and counted *thirteen* drafts of 'Landscape with Freckled Woman'. The final draft was the thirteenth. None of the earlier drafts was a complete draft. Most consisted of a few pages only. I would begin what I hoped was the final draft but would soon become so confused and entangled that I had to begin yet again. I can't recall any other subject costing me so much effort, and the subject might be fairly said to be the place of female personages in the fiction of a fictional character, which subject might be fairly said to reveal something, if only indirectly, of the place of female personages in my own fiction.

My fourth book was not, at first, conceived as any sort of book. What became 'The Battle of Acosta Nu' began as a novel. (I still referred to full-length works of fiction as 'novels' in those days.) 'Sipping the Essence' was written when I was first employed as a teacher of fiction-writing in a college of advanced education in 1980 and found myself required to teach students how to write short stories when I had written none myself. I found it hard to keep my short fiction short, and on a day that I can't recall I decided that my bits and pieces could become a collection, and on another day I decided to link my six pieces in the way that they are now inextricably linked, with each having as its purported author the narrator of the previous piece. The purported author of the first piece is the narrator of 'Landscape with Artist' so that the whole might be called the literary equivalent of a snake swallowing its tail, although this frivolous comment must not suggest that I would ever write a piece of fiction for any but a serious purpose.

In all the years since its publication, I've expected some or another reader of my fourth book to tell me that my way of connecting the six stories was previously devised by a writer unknown to me. No such message has yet reached me, and I now begin to suppose that I'm the inventor of a useful literary device and that someone will one day borrow it from me for his or her own collection.

INLAND

I wanted from an early age to be a poet, but this was not because I considered poetry superior to fiction. I read as much fiction as poetry and was equally affected by both, but my ignorant teachers and the ignorant authors of my textbooks had led me to suppose that an author of fiction is gifted with some sort of insight into human nature, and — more preposterous still — that the purpose of fiction is to create believable characters. I was in my twenties before I learned that I was admirably qualified to write fiction, because I knew next-to-nothing about human nature and was incapable of creating any sort of characters, and I was in my forties before I learned that a certain sort of author may be able to write a work of fiction the meaning of which he himself cannot explicate.

No sound in the English language corresponds to the vowel-sound in the Magyar word *kút*. The vowel-sound in such English words as *moor* or *poor* is vaguely similar, but only vaguely. The Magyar sound is intense and consistent, making it eminently suitable for a singer to inflate and to prolong with feeling. I inflate and prolong the sound thus once at least daily.

Ten years ago, I composed a musical setting for two paragraphs comprising a hundred and fifty-six words in the

Magyar language. The music is my own version of Gregorian chant. Knowing nothing of musical notation, I committed my composition, so to call it, to memory while I was devising it, which took no effort whatever. I likewise committed to memory the two paragraphs mentioned. The word *kút* occurs thrice in the paragraphs, but I prolong its vowel-sound only when I chant it for the third and final time, near the end of the second of the two paragraphs.

The date is surely recorded in the relevant volume of some or another registry of deaths, but the author of the two paragraphs and of the volume of non-fiction surrounding them makes no mention of dates or of names. Given that he saw as a schoolboy what he later wrote about, the year must have been between 1908 and 1916. The season was obviously winter, since ice is mentioned several times in the two paragraphs. The place was a remote landed estate in Tolna County.

Of all the farm-servants on the estate the cowherds were the earliest to begin work, and their first task was to draw water for their animals from the sweep-arm well. On the morning under mention, the cowherds' buckets dragged out a corpse, the remains of a person who would have been known to all those at the well. The Magyar word denoting her has for its English equivalent either *girl* or *young woman*. I know little enough about her. In the second of the two paragraphs, her face is described as beautiful and her nose as having an upwards tilt, giving her a slightly haughty appearance. Certainly, she was of an age and an appearance to have attracted the notice of the man who was responsible, if only indirectly, for her death. This was one of the assistant farm-managers, one of the several layers of men who super-vised the estate on behalf of the absentee landlord. He was by no means unmoved by the death that he had caused. In the text following the two notable paragraphs, he is described as striding up and down near the corpse and beating his riding-crop against his boots, white-faced and agitated.

The book in which these matters are reported has an autobiographical strand throughout but seems mostly to be considered a work of sociology or, perhaps, anthropology, although without the trappings of a scholarly text. The two notable paragraphs, as I call them, are the first paragraphs of a lengthy chapter containing no further mention of the girl who drowned herself. Having described the appearance of the corpse, the author turns to the assistant farm-manager and what might be called the larger social context. The man is described as stout and, by implication, of middle age. His agitation is attributed to the dead girl's having gone against long-standing custom; she has dared to disrupt the general order of things. The English translation of the text, although not the original Magyàr, has a sub-title for each chapter. For the chapter beginning with the two notable paragraphs, the sub-title is *The defencelessness of the girls. The morals of the puszta. The conquerors.*

Who could begin to estimate the number of girls and young women, in Hungary alone, who might have endured what the drowned girl could not endure? Their stories were never told, and hers might never have been told except that one of the group of schoolchildren who paused to view her corpse on that freezing morning before they were sent on their way by the agitated wielder of the riding-crop – one of that little band was Gyula Illyés. The family Illyés never sank quite to the level of poverty that kept the farm-servants on the great estates of Hungary in virtual slavery, and when Gyula was in his teens they escaped to the next-lowest level of their society and the boy obtained a secondary education. But it was not only this that helped to save the drowned girl from oblivion. I once saw a family portrait in which the youngest sitter, a boy of perhaps seven years, looked towards the camera so intensely that I was likely for an instant to drop my own eyes. This was surely the gaze that took in the details on the freezing morning: the gaze under which the uptilted nose kept its haughtiness even after death.

Gyula Illyés wrote no fiction that I'm aware of. He was a prolific poet and the major poet in Hungary by the time of his death in 1983. *People of the Puszta* (*Puszták Népe* in Magyar) is one of a handful of such works written in his early years when he was a political activist, and yet this is Illyés's best-known work outside Hungary, and the English translation of 1971 is one of many such. I first read that translation in 1977. And no, I'm not about to report that I knew even then that the personage who had come to life in my mind would one day find her way into a work of fiction. I've tried to explain already in *this* work that a work of fiction is for me a pattern of meaning that might need many years for its formation. No, what strikes me now is the seeming incongruity of the third-previous sentence; I find it hard to accept that certain images and certain feelings were not always part of my awareness: that I was a thinking and feeling being for nearly forty years without the stark shadow of a sweep-arm well falling every day across my mental vision.

I can't remember how or when I learned to read and write my native English, but I remember writing a euphonious sentence at about the time of my fifth birthday and long before I had started at school. My parents and my two brothers and I had moved recently from Melbourne to Bendigo, and our first home there was a suite of rented rooms at the rear of the house mentioned in the third essay of this collection – the house described as palatial-seeming and having a spacious front garden. The woman of the house was probably in her late thirties at the time. She had a mass of dark hair and a forceful personality. (She was also the mother of one of the girls who invited me to join the game mentioned in the third essay.) That woman was the first person to read the first sentence of mine that I can recall. I believe I wrote the sentence in order to impress her or, perhaps, to repay her for the attention that she directed to me. The sentence was *The bull is full.*

Thirty and more years after I had reached out to the dark-haired landlady, I resolved to compose several thousand sentences for the sake of a dark-haired female personage whose dwelling-place, so to call it, was a passage comprising one hundred and fifty-six words in a language unknown to me. (None of those words, by the way, refers to the hair of the personage. So, why have I asserted that her hair is dark-coloured? In order to answer that question, I would have to leave off writing this essay on the meaning of *Inland* and to begin an essay that would finally explain, as much for my own benefit as for any reader's, why the process of reading a certain sort of text is for me only partly concerned with the text itself: why I can hardly read a certain sort of text without writing simultaneously a text of my own – a profuse, diffuse but near-to-truthful text on some of the countless pages of what Proust's narrator calls the book-in-one's-heart.)

The mention of Proust's narrator just now has reminded me of several passages in which the same personage deplores the many excuses used by writers to avoid confronting their true subject-matter, and the many false tasks undertaken to avoid meeting the demands of their true task. I knew for nearly ten years after reading *People of the Puszta* that I must write a work of fiction in order to understand the meaning for me of that experience. When the time came for me to write what I first thought of as *Hinterland*, I used no excuses, but I undertook at least one false task. The drawer labelled *Inland* in my Literary Archive contains perhaps ten thousand words of various drafts of an opening section set in the editorial office of a magazine titled *Victorian Landscape*. When I looked through these pages just now, I could hardly believe that I once spent many weeks on a task that proved so utterly irrelevant, but the same pages reminded me also that I sensed from the beginning how difficult it would be to uncover the true meaning of the subject-matter of the book now known as *Inland*.

On a certain evening in the winter of 1985, I was walking along Cape Street, Heidelberg, towards the Austin Hospital in order to visit the younger of my brothers, who was seriously ill. I had spent much of the day struggling with the early pages of my book. Not for the first nor for the last time, I found what I had for long needed several hours after I had put away my latest pages and had ceased to think actively about my writing problems. Near the footbridge that crosses

Burgundy Street towards the hospital, I heard myself reciting the words that now comprise the first sentence of *Inland*. I am still able to recall what I felt while I recited: the sensation of having arrived on the inner side of some sort of barrier or wall that had previously seemed impenetrable or insurmountable. The final draft took more than two years to complete, but only because I was fully employed as a teacher of fiction-writing with more than eighty students and because my wife was ill for much of the time — after having passed beyond that barrier or wall, I wrote fluently and confidently. And yet I had to wait until I began to write *these* few pages about *Inland* before I began to understand fully my experience on that winter evening thirty-five years ago.

One of my correspondents during the 1990s, a person whose published literary criticism has shown much insight into my books, sent me in a letter an interpretation of *Inland* that I found mistaken and unjustified. I prepared to send in return a clear explanation of the meaning of a text so often misunderstood. I had not gone far when I found myself confused and struggling for words. When I came to explain how the text appeared to have several narrators but was in fact narrated by the one personage, I found myself defeated. I resorted to the sort of explanation that a child might have devised, a child such as could have composed his first sentence of prose fiction in order to work on the feelings of a handsome female with a mass of dark hair. I asked my correspondent to suppose that a certain sort of writer had tried by every conventional means to draw near to a personage who had first appeared to him while he was reading a book in which were reported her existence and several other matters

53

relating to her. Having thus tried and failed, the writer did what an angry, baffled child or a character in a fairy-story might have done. The child might have daydreamed his way into the setting of the book in the hope of mingling with the characters; the fairy-tale hero might have stepped through a page of text as though through a door to a place where characters were persons after all; the writer used writerly means in his effort to achieve his end.

I've written elsewhere about my having learned the Magyar language when I left the workforce at the age of fifty-five. I was always aware that my explanations for having learned Magyar were tempered to meet the expectations of my readers. Only while I prepared to write this essay, however, did I truly understand my own motives. Whatever I may have said or written about my wanting to read in the original the treasury of Hungarian literature, I truly wanted to read only one book. And no matter what I may have said or written about that admirable evocation of rural hardship, I truly wanted to read only two paragraphs in that book and, in fact, only the second of those two: the paragraph beginning, in English, 'The cowherds pulled her out when they watered the cattle at dawn . . . ' and ending ' . . . dashed straight as an arrow to the well.'

'A csirások húzták ki hajnali itatáskor . . . ' Literally, 'The cowherds pulled-her out dawnish helping-to-drink time . . . ' ' . . . és egy iramban, nyílegyensen a kúthoz rohant.' Literally, 'and one direction-in, arrow-straightishly the well-towards she-dashed.' As I wrote above, I chant at least once daily my own musical setting of these two passages and, of course, the sentences between them. (They are two only, and each is at least as long and complex as any sentence in this essay.) I chant also the short introductory paragraph that stands before the crucial paragraph. A nineteenth-century linguist, after counting the vowels and consonants in samples of every language known to him, declared that Magyar was the most musical-sounding of all. Illyés himself once called his native language 'our exquisite Ugric tongue'. I've told a few persons about my daily chanting. I've probably told them also about the richness of many Magyar vowel-sounds and the denseness of the many compound words. Only when I prepared to write this essay, however, did I truly understand my own motives. Whatever I may have said about the chanted sounds, I value most the vowel-sound in the word *kút*. I hear that sound, sustained by my own breath, when I chant the first sentence of the long paragraph; I hear the sound in the word *húzták*. I hear the sound also in mid-paragraph, when the word *kút* occurs for the first time. The long vowel-sound reverberates thrice like a musical phrase in a symphonic movement. But what I hear is no sort of musical abstraction. What I truly hear persuades me that I've arrived at last at the end of my impossible journey: my delusional, literal-minded enterprise. I have penetrated not only a book and not only a paragraph. I have reached the heart of a word itself. What I hear is a hollow-sounding echo. I am inside the well.

VELVET WATERS

I recall reading, more than fifty years ago, a complaint by Jorge Luis Borges that the traditional novel had no *shape* that could be apprehended or appreciated by the general reader, whereas the shape of a short story could be readily grasped and admired. I read in 1962 some of the first of Borges's works to be translated into English and was much impressed, although I can't recall any urge to write his sort of fiction. And yet, in the late 1960s, when I was preparing to write *Tamarisk Row*, the first draft of which comprised eventually some 180,000 words, my notes included an elaborate chart or diagram: a foolscap page covered with numbered squares. Each square contained both a red and a green numeral. The red numerals were sequential, and their only purpose was to identify the squares, which numbered 220. The green numerals seemed to have been distributed at random among the squares, and they were rather fewer than a hundred, so that the same numeral often appeared in two or more widely scattered squares. Each red numeral identified what I called a *section* of my still unwritten book. (Most of my fiction, whether book-length or shorter, I've envisaged beforehand as comprising *sections* − never *chapters*, which word suggests to me a temporal or logical sequence.)

The significance of the green numerals was explained in a document titled The Master List and kept in the same folder that contained the numbered chart. The Master List comprised about 7,000 words arranged in long paragraphs each of which defined in detail one or another so-called *theme*.

If the folder mentioned above contained only what I've described so far, then my planning for my first book of fiction would seem to have been straightforward and purposeful, if overly detailed, but the folder contains much else: seeming evidence that I envisaged at times a work rather different in structure from that which was finally written.

I wonder whether I recalled Borges's complaint at any time during the months when I was trying to devise an intricate shape for my excessively long first work. Memories of complex projects that I planned, if not executed, in my childhood suggest that I was always attracted to complexity and orderliness and driven to represent visually these and other seeming-abstractions. Not only have I no recollection of my being inspired or driven by Borges's statement, but I've never forgotten the day when my lighting on the device of the numbered squares seemed to assure me that I would complete, sooner or later, the task that had so often seemed beyond me. The numbered squares, so I've always believed, derived from my having often in mind beforehand an image of a page of the calendar mentioned in the very first section of *Tamarisk Row*. Almost every work of fiction of mine has seemed to grow from a central image, and the yellowish numbered squares below the sombre-toned paintings of Biblical subjects had been for long suggestive of the family Killeaton's traversing the

57

sunlit city of Bassett, overhung by scenes from their ever-present religious mythology.

I need hardly report that I gave up trying to follow the chart long before I had finished the first draft of the text, but only because I had grossly underestimated the wordage needed to enlarge on my so-called themes. The plan that I had drawn up was unworkable, but I kept to the concept. The themes, as I called them, are interwoven. The ninety-six carefully arranged sections of the published text of *Tamarisk Row* are still a shapely whole although not the elaborate pattern that I had once designed.

Each of the four sections of *A Season on Earth* has its own shape, although not such as required a diagram for its planning. The shape of the fourth and last section includes a miniature version of the shape of the whole. Adrian, during a few hectic weeks, relives in daydreams each of his earlier quests, so to call them. He fixes his hopes, yet again but briefly, on one after the other of sexual pleasure, romantic love, the priesthood, and poetry before losing his last hold on reality and seeing himself, perhaps, as fit only to survive within the covers of a book rather than in the actual world.

The text now published as *The Plains* may be one of the few longer pieces that I've written with little thought for its shape. (I took much care, however, with what might be called the narrative framework – every statement in the text is made by a narrator who reviews events from the twenty years before the beginning of the narration itself.) Yet *The Only Adam*, the still unpublished long work from which the published work was extracted, was intended to have a complex shape indeed. I spent several weeks preparing an intricate diagram, the four parts of which were linked, in turn, to the face, the breasts, the pubic region, and the mind/soul of a hypothetical female personage. When I looked again at the diagram just now, for the first time in thirty years and more, I could not believe that a published author once hoped to be guided in his writing by such a labyrinth, as my diagram seems now. I wonder whether the deviser of the diagram had wanted to use it, paradoxically, to liberate rather than restrict him. Perhaps he hoped that his pondering on the underlying shape of his still-unwritten work would guide him whenever he later had to select from a welter of unlooked-for images and feelings. Perhaps he hoped that after dwelling on the excessive details of an unworkable scheme, he would be enabled to put together a much simplified version.

The previous paragraphs beg the questions, what sort of shape is under discussion? how can such a shape be visualised or compared with similar shapes? how can such a shape be described in words or diagrammatically? My answers to such questions seem barely adequate even to me. I seem to think of my book-length works of fiction as being too substantial to be represented by anything other than extensive charts or diagrams with much breadth and depth but no other dimension. My shorter works, however, present themselves to me sometimes as three-dimensional *structures*, often transparent and containing further sorts of complexity.

Whenever I read or look into 'When the Mice Failed to Arrive', the first piece in the collection *Velvet Waters*, I feel that the whole has a shape deserving to be called *appropriate* or *satisfying* or even *admirable*, even though I struggle to visualise that shape.

I can go some way towards defining that shape and justifying its appeal to me. The two major elements that give the piece its shape are what most persons would call *time* and *place* or, more properly, *fictional time* and *fictional place*. If the piece had been narrated more conventionally, I could have measured its timespan, which is to say that I could have measured the time from the earliest action reported to the latest. But the piece purports to be only a report of memories and daydreams; the narrator recalls a few events from a single afternoon at some time before the writing of the text as well as a host of remembered or conjectured events. Complications abound. It would be difficult, but not at all impossible, to consider as one series all the differing kinds of events and to meas- ure the span from earliest to latest. I prefer to distinguish between the remembered afternoon in the narrator's suburban house and all the other periods of time that he remembers in connection with that one afternoon and to find what follows from the distinction. It happens, for example, that the events of the one afternoon are reported in fewer than a thousand words while the assortment of memories, so to call them, are reported in more than nine thousand. One notable feature of the shape of the piece is thus established: its irregularity. Memories of one kind seem to overhang or overshadow the other kind. From the sense of imbalance comes the threat of overturning – or, has such an overturning taken place already? So, the shape of the piece is no simple outline but a many-sided entity with varying densities and such qualities, perhaps, as translucence or transparence or opacity. In this connection, the two scenes, so to call them, in the suburban house seem in my mind more brightly lit and more solid than most other episodes. The varying luminescence may be caused also by the many references to clouds and smoke and restricting grilles or meshes.

If a doubtful reader were to assert that the shape I've assigned to my piece of fiction is an arbitrary, unverifiable thing with no existence outside my own mind, I would not attempt to refute him or her. My trying to describe or define such a thing as the *shape* of a piece of fiction is my notion of what others call literary criticism or book reviewing. I know of no better way to appraise a work of fiction than to observe and then to report for one's own benefit, or for others', the extent to which the reading of the work has changed the set of one's mind.

In earlier years, I would sometimes feel annoyed by the unpredictability of my writing processes. I never discovered an effective, foolproof method for planning and then bringing to completion a coherent, meaningful work of fiction. Every piece that I was driven to write, whatever its length, seemed to require a different preparation and a different execution. I believe it was the writing of 'Precious Bane' in 1985 that persuaded me my writing methods were not haphazard or poorly organised. I had already been telling my students for five years that my sort of writer looked not outwards but inwards for subject-matter. I quoted often the statement by an American writer that one should trust one's obsessions. I took a surprisingly long time to develop confidence not only in the contents of my mind but in the means by which those contents reveal themselves.

I've sometimes said that I wrote 'Precious Bane' during a single weekend. When I looked into my Literary Archive

61

just then, I learned that this was an exaggeration. What I wrote during a single weekend was a draft that needed rewriting only once to become the final draft. What deserves to be reported is that I wrote the first paragraphs of my first draft without making any sort of notes beforehand. What I had in mind when I began the draft was the sort of puzzle that has often led me to write fiction with much meaning. I had been puzzled for some time by feelings of gloom and uneasiness the source of which I could not identify. The feelings had first overcome me in a certain second-hand bookshop, and what seemed to give rise to them is made clear in the published text. So, the contents of the piece might be said to have risen successively to view in the once-mysterious background behind the image of a grey-faced man standing among dusty bookshelves. This account of things explains why 'Precious Bane' has for me a shape distinctive but hard to describe: a long series of images receding into the background, with each image rendered visible only through the fading or dissolving of the image in front of it.

Mention of dissolving imagery brings to mind 'First Love', the second-last piece in *Velvet Waters*. So many complexities are denoted by its ten thousand words of text that I could not hope to visualise its shape, although I sometimes suppose that a person skilled in draughtsmanship or modelling could find the means to represent its intricacy. The task might prove less difficult if the artist or craftsman could accept the proposition of the narrator of 'First Love' that time and place are one and the same. I sometimes glimpse a dome of bluish or lilac-coloured glass enclosing a cluster of landscapes somehow resembling the atomic structure of some complex molecule.

Dissolving imagery recalls also the claim by the narrator of *Inland* that every thing is more than one thing. It recalls too the claim that I've several times made in my own person of how the greater part of the contents of *Inland* was revealed to me in a flash after I had recognised that a fishpond in a backyard of a suburb of Melbourne was also a well on a remote country estate in Hungary. And if any reader of this essay should consider fanciful the contents of this and the previous paragraph, then I can assure the reader that I have a similar experience when I try to read most reviews of fiction and most scholarly articles. The reading of a work of fiction alters – sometimes briefly but sometimes permanently – the configuration of my mental landscape and augments the number of personages who are its temporary or permanent residents. Morality, social issues, psychological insight – such matters seem as fanciful and inconsequential to me as my talk of shapes and dissolving imagery might seem to my conjectured reader.

When a piece of short fiction has sometimes resisted my efforts to visualise its shape, I've tried instead to see in mind an image, whether simple or complex, that deserves to be called its *central* image. Mention of centrality implies at once the sort of shape possessed by a solar system or a galaxy, and this in turn brings with it a certain reassurance; it's surely comforting to be allowed to suppose that mental imagery uncovered after much effort displays patterns clearly evident in the visible universe. And for all that I've written so far about the shape of this or that piece of fiction, I'm still able to visualise, at the heart of almost every shape, a central image; for 'When the Mice Failed to Arrive' a timid, bewhiskered mouse looking outwards from behind a grey mesh; for 'Precious Bane' a greyness criss-crossed by a network of gold-coloured pathways; for 'First Love' a zone of blue caught in the process of changing to lilac.

A certain sort of reader of these paragraphs might have cause to complain that an author of my sort denies him or her what readers of fiction have traditionally sought and obtained: meetings-up with complex but credible characters; insights into human nature. My reply to such a complaint would be the claim that the alert reader of my fiction obtains therefrom an extraordinarily detailed knowledge of its implied narrator, the personage who created it. The mouse behind the mesh, the grey-gold monastery/brain, and the sky of the melting colours – each of these and of the host of their counterparts throughout my fiction is an item of evidence, no matter how fragmentary, of the workings of the mysterious invisible entity that we call Mind.

EMERALD BLUE

During my long lifetime, I've fallen in love with several hundred female personages and persons. The personages, of course, could never be expected even to be aware of my existence. Many of the persons were likewise unaware, and of the remainder, many would never have been aware of my feelings towards them. Of the small number still unaccounted for, a mere handful seemed to return my feelings, and of that handful I drew close to only two or three, depending on one's definition of *closeness*.

I no longer feel for the persons as I formerly felt. (If the narrator of À *la recherche du temps perdu* is to be believed, then the feelings themselves have been preserved and might assert themselves yet again under certain conditions.) Matters are far different, however, with the personages. Some I seem to have forgotten, together with the texts that first made me aware of their existence. But the many that I'm still aware of still keep their hold on me, and of these I feel most warmly for Emily Brontë.

She bears the name of a person who was once flesh and blood, but in my scheme of things she whom I most regard derives much of her nature from a fictional personage named Catherine Earnshaw and part of her appearance from an actual person who was fourteen years of age when I first read *Wuthering Heights* and who last spoke with me in the following year, which was 1957. (No one should be allowed to write without explanation a statement such as comprises the second of the co-ordinated main clauses in the previous sentence, as though fictional reports of words and deeds denote fictional natures or characters beyond dispute. I have not read *Wuthering Heights* for nearly sixty years, but I have not forgotten my reading a certain passage allowing me to bring into being a personage for whom, at the end of her fictional life, a certain feather torn from the pillow on her deathbed is means enough for her to recall a certain ground-dwelling bird and its desolate habitat, which had been the place of refuge for herself and the person closest to her when they were both children.) What took place while I read was no sort of learning or interpretation: no sort of extraction from words whatever might have been their agreed meaning. I doubt whether I made any sort of decision. I simply witnessed an event such as I had hoped might be possible since I first taught myself to read and write.

Neither *Velvet Waters* nor *Emerald Blue* had been intended as a book. For some time after the publication of *Inland* in 1988, I had been preparing to write a substantial, book-length work of fiction titled *O, Dem Golden Slippers*, although I wrote little of the text itself until early 1990. Believing that my next long work would take several years to write, I had set about collecting, as early as 1988, the various short works of mine published in periodicals during the previous decade. After I had written the longish title-piece in early 1990, I had all that was needed for my sixth book and plenty of time, so I thought, to write *O, Dem Golden Slippers*.

I had written perhaps a third of a near-to-final draft of my latest work when I decided to abandon it and, moreover, to give up writing fiction for the time being, if not for good. I told very few people, and I don't recall what reasons, if any, I gave for my decision. I told no one my true reason, although I told it to my wife after a year or two. I did, however, make two attempts to write a piece of fiction suggesting or explaining why I had abandoned the enterprise that had been my chief task for thirty years. The first was 'The Interior of Gaaldine', and the second, more than ten years later, was *Barley Patch*, which was also meant to impart what might have been imparted by *O, Dem Golden Slippers* if I had completed it.

My wife had been disappointed to learn that I was writing no more fiction, and it was partly her urging that persuaded me to write 'Emerald Blue' and 'In Far Fields' in an effort to get together a collection similar to *Velvet Waters*. I needed no persuading, however, to begin 'The Interior of Gaaldine'. I had put into writing in 1985 the first details of the imaginary horse-racing that I now call the Antipodean Archive. For several years, those details were enclosed in a few manila folders and I had no wish to reveal their existence to anyone although, as I wrote above, I told my wife about them eventually. I privately considered my horse-racing landscapes as important and as fulfilling as I had formerly considered my fiction-writing, but I lacked for some time the confidence to declare this to others.

It was a seeming-coincidence that I read, at about this time, a biography of the Brontë family by Juliet Barker. I had known for many years of the Brontës' imagined world, so to call it, but I learned numerous details from the biography. I seem to have learned also, at about that time, to feel no unease for having brought into being such a place as my Antipodes. (The name is a general term for the two independent nations of New Arcady and New Eden.) If scholars speculated on the implications of Gondal and Gaaldine and the connections of those places with their founders' literary works, I should surely consider my own creations as serious an enterprise as any other collection of folders in either of my other archives.

I was heartened, too, by certain correspondences. The Brontës' two lands were located, as were mine, in the South Pacific, although my creation lay far to the south of theirs. The casual-seeming jotting by Emily, 'Gondal is discovering the interior of Gaaldine', has always suggested to me that events in her other world must often have occupied her during her daily routine somewhat as I've been intruded on since early childhood by images of horse-races in no place on Earth. And only days after beginning to learn the Hungarian language, I seemed to have been sent a reassuring coded message when I learned that *gondol* means *he or she thinks*.

That same jotting, as I've called it, has often set me thinking of the similarities or otherwise between what is called *time* in the world where I sit writing this sentence and several other scales of measurement, so to call them, for intervals between perceived events reported (or left unreported) in works of fiction. I've always understood Emily's note as a sort of reminder to herself that some of the citizenry of Gondal, whether or not she would ever report the matter or would even learn more than a few of its details, were engaged in a momentous enterprise – the discovery of a land supplementary to their own. The brevity of the note has always told me that Emily is content not to alter the situation as I've reported it in the previous sentence; she may never try to call to mind more than a few details, let alone to report them in writing. No matter! Gondal no longer needs her validation or supervision. The Gondals, as I've sometimes seen them named, are free to experience, far from prying writers or readers, their own equivalents of our joys and sorrows.

In my early years as a writer of fiction, I believed I should never be called on to explain or clarify the meaning, so to call it, of any published item of mine, and I was ready to decline to do so, if asked. I believed that the text itself was all that should be required from me. Like all resolutions, mine was made to be broken, and I've not hesitated to break it whenever I've volunteered to put my own interpretation on certain passages for readers of good will, as I call them. And, as I reported in my essay on *Inland*, I was no more able than my readers to clarify certain matters.

I don't find this strange today. Little of what I've written is the product of reasonable thought or of a clear-eyed inspection of what most call the world and I call the visible world. Most of what I've written is the product of intense feeling and an instinctive, hasty selection from the host of images generated by that feeling. And so it was with my report of the scene, so to call it, in the hotel room at Devonport early in 'The Interior of Gaaldine'. What I wrote was as faithful an account as I could deliver of what I saw in mind. I can't put the matter more simply. Why I saw in mind what I saw would be impossible for me to explain, even if I cared to try. I might explain that I've heard in mind countless times the knocking sound that I first heard when I read, in 1956, the passage in which Lockwood hears such a sound while he sleeps in what was Catherine's bedroom. And I might say that having heard that sound yet again while I sat at my desk on a certain day thirty-six years later, I understood that the person knocking would give her name as 'Ellis' (heard by the narrator as 'Alice') and would resemble the only portrait I had seen of Emily Brontë. But more than that is not for me to say. If 'The Interior of Gaaldine' purported to be a different sort of fiction, then a reader might be entitled to ask whether the narrator was dreaming or hallucinating or whether his visitor was a clever imposter, but my fiction is none of that.

To say, as I've said often in recent years, that I write fiction by reporting the contents of my mind is to explain nothing. Nor would I take what seems the easy way around the matter by declaring that my fiction is the product of something called the *imagination*. The word *envisage* is useful. The same word is also unpretentious, and I use it sometimes from a fear of seeming in any way pretentious. Mostly I refer simply to *fictional events* and *fictional personages*, hoping thus to prevent my fiction from being taken as a report of things that once happened in the world where I sit as I write it or even of things that *may* have happened there.

So, a fictional female personage calling herself, perhaps, 'Ellis' knocks by night at the door of a fictional male person-age for the purpose of delivering to him the detailed records purporting to have been compiled during his lifetime of races contested by horses known only to the solitary compiler on racecourses known likewise only to him. The outcome of each race, and the many details contributing thereto, have been determined by the occurrence of certain letters in passages of prose chosen at random from books of literary fiction. (For reasons that the narrator cannot fathom, the most suitable books for this purpose are those first published in the nineteenth century.) No thoughtful reader of the fiction thus summarised could help but speculate as to what might be called the deeper meaning. My guess is that most such readers would suppose that the writer of the fiction had that meaning in mind while he wrote. I hereby assure those readers that the writer had not.

Of course, I had in mind a certain sort of meaning, but as any thoughtful writer is surely aware, the actual process of writing true fiction cannot be planned beforehand with any certainty. (I call *my* sort of writing *true fiction*, but other writers also write it.) Ideas can be noted beforehand; summaries can be made; themes, strands, or elements can be listed; whole patterns of these things can be visualised. What finds its way onto the page is always unexpected, sometimes hugely so.

After having written the previous paragraph, I looked into the drawer labelled *Emerald Blue* in my Literary Archive. The earliest item among the hanging files labelled 'The Interior of Gaaldine' is a manila folder titled 'Early Notes and Jottings, 1989–1993'. The folder contains about forty pages, each with fewer than a hundred words in the barely legible scrawl that I tend to use when I'm trying to record thoughts that have come to me in haste. Of the several pages that I read, none seemed connected in any way with the published text. My having found and read those notes reminds me of how confused and uncertain I've been for most of the many months and years that I've spent on the early drafts of my books. My mood overall was mostly confident. The imagery and the feelings that had compelled me to begin writing – these could be trusted, but not everything that had seemed at first to be a part of their constellation was truly so.

I believe today that I was driven to write 'The Interior of Gaaldine' partly to reassure myself that my Antipodean Archive, as I mostly call it nowadays, is as worthy a task as was the planning and writing of any of my published works and I believe that my reassurance came largely from my scant knowledge of the life of Emily Brontë and my even scantier knowledge of her Gondal and Gaaldine. I assert this today, but a year hence, and in different circumstances, I might feel compelled to account for my having included in the piece the paragraphs about Thomas Merton or my having set the piece, so to speak, in Tasmania. And this uncertainty on my part seems to justify my long-ago belief that I should keep silent about my published writing. I thought long ago that the meaning of a published text could be discovered from a study of the text alone. I thought in somewhat the way that thinkers in earlier times thought about atoms and molecules.

I might well have included in one or another of the preceding few paragraphs a claim made by the narrator of 'In Far Fields', the first piece in *Emerald Blue*. I've always been especially proud of this piece and of the first few pages in particular. I myself never delivered as a teacher to any student or students such a detailed account of my writing methods as the narrator claims to have delivered, but nothing in the narrator's account goes against any of my beliefs about my writing, and my career as an author of fiction might have gone rather more smoothly if I had had some of his seeming confidence and if I had been able to follow faithfully his instructions for writing fiction of meaning. One claim of his has stayed with me since I read the piece recently: his claim that all the images in his mind are in their rightful places.

For much of the time while I wrote this essay, I thought otherwise about my mental imagery. Certainly the imagery was mostly arranged in constellations, as I call them, but it seemed to me that the process of writing itself helped, partly at least, to assign certain constellations to their foredestined positions. (And my using today the word *constellations* will not prevent me tomorrow from thinking of townships on a mental map.) If I thought of my writing as more a disclosing or uncovering than a fabrication, would the task itself be rather different or rather easier? Like the narrator, I've often placed much trust in my judgement when I've shuffled folders or sheets of paper in an effort to arrive at a sequence of sections that would create a shapely whole from parts not easy to combine or connect. I've even enjoyed a peculiar satisfaction, difficult indeed to describe, when a sort of unity has appeared from the bringing together of seeming opposites. Did this satisfaction come from my adding a new detail to an incomplete map or from my learning at last what had for long been in place?

Finally, in the weeks before I began this essay, I wrote notes on more than twenty system cards. While I was actually writing this essay, I referred to no more than a half-dozen of the cards. The rest are about to be bundled up and stored in the file labelled *Discarded* in the drawer labelled *Last Letter to a Reader* in my Literary Archive. I wonder where in my scheme of things are the images that I had in mind while I wrote on all those cards.

INVISIBLE YET
ENDURING LILACS

Invisible Yet Enduring Lilacs is called a collection of essays, but this convenient classification covers over some inconsistencies. 'Stream System', for example, had previously been included in *Velvet Waters*, which presents itself, of course, as a collection of short fiction. 'Birds of the Puszta' was meant to be a book review. 'Meetings with Adam Lindsay Gordon' and several other items were commissioned articles for literary periodicals or newspaper supplements. 'Pure Ice' was at first the speech that I wrote and delivered for the launch of *Inland* at the Adelaide Festival in 1988. (And here, now, is my chance to correct an error that has troubled me often during the twenty-five years since I became aware of it. My having made the error in the first place is yet more evidence that my reading – and not just the reading of fiction, but any sort of reading – is no search for facts or truths but rather an endless quest for elements in my unique mythology. My meeting-up with the female personage mentioned in the fifth of these essays was sufficiently momentous to have blurred for me much else that I learned from the pages nearby. I declared to my audience in Adelaide that I had never been able to suppose that a certain young woman had been able to read, even in the language of ghosts, any pages of mine. A few years later, after I had read a second time what had become blurred during my first reading, I understood that the young woman would have been able to read any pages that she chose to read in the Magyar language. Each estate-owner in the Kingdom of Hungary was obliged by law to provide an elementary school for the children of workers on the estate. Gyula Illyés had filled six pages of his book with accounts of his schooldays on Rácegres Puszta – pages that had become blurred after I had read a certain other page of the same book.) As for the long piece that gives my book its title, it was delivered in 1989 as one of a series of lectures to meagre audiences in an obscure art gallery. (The other lectures, none of which I attended, were on such subjects as de Chirico, New Wave Cinema, and Heidegger.) I had begun the text for the lecture by recording noteworthy thoughts of mine while I read, for the third and final time, the Scott Moncrieff translation of À *la recherche du temps perdu*. This, of course, is the same method that I've used to write the essays in this present collection – while re-reading each of my published books, I make a note of certain thoughts that occur to me. I'm hardly interested in recurring or predictable thoughts but I'm eager to follow up the unsought-for and the seemingly incongruous.

I can't recall why I wrote an author's note for the first book of mine to be published for ten years, but I suppose I was somewhat uncomfortable with the appearance of the word 'Essays' on the title page. While I had been writing the last two of the thirteen items in the collection, I could have thought of no more apt word for them, but some of the others were hybrids indeed, and not only on account of what had happened to them before their publication in a book of essays.

'Stream System', as I've reported already, was published in a collection of short fiction fifteen years before its inclusion among the essays in *Invisible Yet Enduring Lilacs*. Thirteen years later again Farrar, Straus and Giroux saw fit to include 'Stream System' in a collection of my short fiction and even to use its title for the book as a whole. At the same time, Giramondo, my Sydney publisher, allowed 'Stream System' into their parallel volume, my *Collected Short Fiction*. This was, in fact, not quite a parallel edition. Whereas the American publisher had conveniently re-classified 'Invisible Yet Enduring Lilacs' as fiction, Giramondo declined to do so.

Does any of this matter greatly? If a prestigious publishing house is prepared to publish as fiction what was previously called an essay, has the Order of Things been violated? Likewise, if another such publisher re-classifies one of my essays but not another from the same collection, so what? I believe today that my last statement in the author's note borders on the flippant. Overjoyed, perhaps, at seeing a book of mine published after ten years of near-retirement, I seem to have cared little as to how my writing was classified. I believe today that I overlooked an important distinction when I wrote the author's note. The borderline pieces, so to call them, were first written as lectures or essays and were later considered by some editors to be fiction. I can't think of any piece of mine that underwent the reverse process: that I wrote as fiction but was later able to consider otherwise.

While I was composing the previous paragraph, I devised and carried out a simple experiment. I supposed that I had been asked to write a piece of short fiction the setting of which was some or another suburb of Melbourne. I then observed my thoughts and feelings as I prepared to begin writing the piece. Afterwards, I likewise observed myself preparing to write an essay inspired, so to speak, by some or another suburb. I observed two notable differences. While I prepared for the fiction, I felt what I've usually felt at such times: I felt obliged to compose something worthy of the attention of the personage I know only as my Ideal Reader. While I prepared for the essay, my conjectured readership was to my liking: a select band of those that I call readers of good will. She whom I call my Ideal Reader, however, was far from my thoughts.

The experiment, as I've called it, brought to my mind also the personage called by Proust *le moi profond*. While I could never be persuaded that I'm the possessor of something deserving to be called an unconscious, Proust's phrase, from the time when I first read it, has seemed the best possible name for the part of me most responsible for my fiction but not always present during other sorts of writing.

I've arrived by a roundabout route at the true subject of *this* essay. I declare often that I've read few passages of fiction more moving than the report towards the end of À *la recherche du temps perdu* of the narrator's standing on the uneven paving-stones. Yet, I suspect that I value Proust's fiction for reasons peculiarly my own and that I disregard most of what others admire in it.

Somewhere in my Chronological Archive, if only I could put my hands on them, are the notes that I used when I was a member of a panel discussing Proust at a session of the Melbourne Writers Festival in one of the earliest years of this century. In fact, the notes might be of little use to me today; I made scant reference to them during the panel's discussions. Much of what I said that day was composed on the spot in a sort of rage that overcame me after I had met up with one of the other members of the panel. I had never heard of him or his recently published and well-received book on Proust, but I took an instant dislike to both after the person chairing the panel-session had seemed to recommend the man to the audience as a sort of generous missionary ready to share the rich insights of a cultured European with us deprived colonials. Before he had uttered a word as a member of the panel, I had decided he was a dilettante and a literary snob: incapable of original judgements but skilled enough with words to be able to paraphrase the common-place judgements of others of their kind on writers already acknowledged as great.

Whenever I've spoken without notes to an audience or whenever I've had to answer questions without notice, the effort to find the right words has always put me into a sort of trance from which I've later emerged with little or no memory of what was said by myself or others. Even my notes, if I could find them, would tell me only what I had *planned* to say rather than what I actually said after I had decided to provoke my fellow-panellist. But if what I actually said has been for long forgotten, I can still recall much of what I *planned* to say during the last few minutes before I was asked to speak. I planned to say a little about myself as I was early in my twenty-second year, when I first read the paperback titled *Swann's Way* and when the English version of Proust's fiction saved me from despair.

I am not exaggerating. The sixty years that have passed since I lived in the rented room with gas-ring and shared bathroom at the rear of 50 Wheatland Road, Malvern, counted for nothing a few weeks ago when I parked my car near the corner of Tooronga Road and walked slowly past the double-fronted brick Edwardian house in what is now a fashionable precinct. With no effort whatever, I became again the young primary-school teacher with no money, no car, no girl-friend, nothing published, and little hope of remedying any of these deprivations. It would have seemed quite in order for me to open the wrought-iron gate and to stride down the driveway towards the place that had seemed to promise much when I first moved in but had soon lost its look of being the place where I first came into my own as a writer. What I struggled to write in that narrow space was mostly poetry, although some of what I entered in the book that I called my journal suggests that I thought sometimes of attempting a novel, as I would have called it then. When I wasn't trying to write, I was reading, but little of what I read seemed of any help. Most of it had been written on the other side of the world by people whose pedigrees and upbringing had destined them to be writers, so I thought. I had already, if only I could have understood the matter, the material for half a dozen works of fiction. I had knelt often, ten or twelve years before, on the threadbare rug in a rented weatherboard cottage in Bendigo, pushing glass marbles around a pretend-racecourse and seeing the pretend-landscape around the course merge into a landscape brought to mind by the hot gusts outside the house of the wind from the plains to the north, where I had never been. I stood often on the cliff-tops above what is now marked on maps as Murnane's Bay, staring northwards across the last few paddocks on the southern edge of the continent towards the stone house where lived my father's parents and four of their five unmarried children, from whom I learned that my first obligation was to the God of the Jansenists and that the way of life most likely to appease Him was that of virginity.

Swann's Way, too, had been written on the far side of the world, and I felt during my first reading of the work what I feel even more surely today: that I could never wish to meet in person the author Marcel Proust. I mean, of course, the *breathing author*. To the implied author, the personage responsible for the text, I could surely confide my gratitude, needing few words to explain how he first encouraged me to undertake my own journey of discovery and to pay heed to what I later learned to call the detail that winks.

The man Marcel, years later, uncovered the mystery of what had perplexed his younger self; of why the sight of a certain flower or the sound of a name on a map seemed linked to such a weight of feeling. The man, years later, saw at last, in the words of one of his biographers, that door fly open at which, before him, no one had knocked. I myself, in that cramped room where I ate from cans and urinated into the sink and spent whole weekends talking to no one, learned from certain passages of *Swann's Way* how to look out for what I later came to call the detail that winked: the one significant detail from among the many that appeared to me while I wrote.

As I wrote above, I recalled afterwards little of what I said about Proust during the panel-discussion at the writers festival, but the import of what I said must have been clear to some at least of the audience and even perhaps to the man who had seemed to me, rightly or wrongly, a bloated parasite on the body of literature. A few at least of those present must have understood my claim that a certain sort of writer deserves as much gratitude as is given to heroes of discovery in other fields, not excluding science or medicine, and that a certain sort of writing can be a matter of life and death.

I read again and again during 1961 certain passages from my brownish-coloured paperback edition of *Swann's Way*. After having sometimes despaired of finding subject-matter peculiarly my own, I was now hopeful, if not confident. (Three more years were to pass before I wrote the first of the notes that led me to write *Tamarisk Row*.) I felt the beginnings of the assurance that I would never cease to feel after the day, twelve years later, when I read, in a later section of Proust's work, a reference to the book being written continually on one's heart, after which day I had always ready the words to describe the true source of all true fiction.

Not all of my accounts of the process of fiction-writing use borrowed words. I can't remember when I first used the expression *the detail that winks*. I may well have devised it while I was writing the lecture that later became 'The Breathing Author' in my eighth published book. Even today, I'm able to get from that expression of mine an assurance that the book in my heart is no mere chronicle but a subtly graduated register in which numerous possible patterns might be discerned. I first delivered the lecture mentioned at a conference of scholars in 2001, when I had written nothing for publication for seven years and had no wish to do so in future. Soon after the lecture, I was questioned closely by the principal of Giramondo Publishing as to what exactly I meant by my talk of winking details. I've never since raised the matter with him, but I've always since supposed that my insights into such things helped to bring us together as the author and the publisher of six further books of mine that might not otherwise have been written.

BARLEY PATCH

He appears to me to have had a very sad and possibly unful-
filled life. His last teacher described him as the brightest
pupil he ever taught. He left school early to work on the farm
but continued to educate himself with extensive reading. He
loved music and regularly listened to ABC broadcasts. He
could talk endlessly.

Although he never married, he was walking out, as they
used to say, with at least three young ladies during his twenties and thirties but none of it came to anything. I suspect
he felt he was needed at home to care for his mother and his
unmarried sisters, who were in poor health. In his later years
he suffered severely from migraine and, possibly, depression,
and there were days when he was unable to work. He was
found to have stomach cancer in 1977 and died soon afterwards at the age of fifty-six.

The previous two paragraphs are an abridgement from a
family history written and privately published by a male
cousin of mine. The man described in the paragraphs was
my youngest uncle and the youngest uncle also of my cousin.
I had the man in mind while I wrote 'Cotters Come No More'.
I wrote about him several times in *Something for the Pain*.

(The book being a memoir, I was able to report the impressions made on me by an actual man rather than a fictional personage.) I had the man in mind continually while I wrote at least three extensive passages in the second half, roughly speaking, of *Barley Patch*. The first such passage begins on page 110 of the first edition and is titled '*What would have been others of those imagined events?*' And I could not have written one of the pieces of fiction that I'm most proud of, 'Last Letter to a Niece', if I had not had in mind my youngest uncle in his twenty-eighth year, when he lived alone in two rooms of what had been the family home before the death of his father and the removal of his mother and his sisters to Warrnambool and when he would have heard from his bed on clear nights the waves of the Southern Ocean breaking on the cliffs just beyond the boundary of the farm.

In the first paragraph of the fifth essay in this collection, I reported my belief as a beginning writer that fiction could be written only by someone with deep insight into human nature. (On page 27 of *Barley Patch*, the narrator reports 'Already, as a very young man, I understood that I might be capable of writing fiction without having first observed numerous interesting places and persons . . . ' This passage, however, is part of a work of fiction.) That was a narrow view of fiction indeed, and I soon learned to think otherwise and to make use of some of the countless possibilities available to the fiction-writer. After the first few of my books had been published, I was emboldened to say sometimes that I wrote fiction for the very reason that I was ignorant: that I had seldom travelled, had observed little, and found human nature baffling. Whenever I tried to put my position to students of my fiction-writing course, I found support from an unlikely quarter. I had never wanted to read anything by Evelyn Waugh, and what little I had read about the man himself repelled me. Yet I enjoyed quoting often his remark to the effect that he had never felt the least inclination to question *why* his characters behaved as they did, much less to write about their motives in his fiction.

Even as a teacher of fiction-writing, I tried to avoid discussions about such matters as whether or not a certain fictional character was *believable* or *convincing*. I never saw any class member persuaded to change his or her mind as a result of such a discussion. Sometimes, however, while I was assessing a piece of fiction, I studied my own reactions while reading about some or another character. (In later years, I came to use the term *fictional personage*.) I developed a rule-of-thumb, so to call it, in which the key words were *conceivable* and its opposite, *inconceivable*. A fictional personage was less than convincing if he or she did or said or thought something that I found inconceivable. That 'something' might never yet have been done or said or thought of, but I might still find it conceivable or possible. If not, the personage responsible for it was less than convincing, which might have been another way of declaring that I denied the personage the right to exist in my mind.

My rule-of-thumb seemed somewhat problematic when I set it out just now, but it was mostly useful, and to the occasional student who was aggrieved by its seeming arbitrariness I could always reply that I was paid by my employer to do things that might well seem arbitrary to others. But most discussion about characters in fiction, convincing or otherwise, seems to me somewhat artificial. Most such discussion seems to assume that the author somehow *creates* or *imagines* or *brings into being* the entities called characters. I myself am not aware of having done any such thing.

Whenever I write so much as a sentence of a work of fiction, I seem to be *reporting*, and that word is one that I make much use of. Mostly I report something that I *see in mind*, and that expression also is one that I make much use of. Much of what I report I seem to have seen for long in mind, but much, too, seems to have appeared in mind shortly before its being reported. When I report such things as memories, longings, daydreams, ambitions, or the like, they are always such as might be attributable to a male person of my time and place. That person is mostly he whom I call the breathing author or the flesh-and-blood author of the fiction. The exceptions are the man who was my father, Reginald Thomas Murnane (1904–1960) and his youngest brother, Louis James Murnane (1921–1977). From this it might well be inferred that I've known only two persons so well that I've dared to report a few of the contents of their own minds with the same assurance that allows me to report my own. What might not be so readily inferred is that I've felt when writing with my uncle in mind rather more assurance than I've felt in connection with my father.

The publisher of *Barley Patch* once described as *amazing* two scenes, so to call them, from the section beginning on page 110 of the first edition. In the first scene, a boy aged about thirteen years imagines himself as clutching at a mass of dark hair that hangs from the head of a young woman who looks down from an upper-storey window. The prince in the fairy-story is able to climb the young woman's hair and to meet with her in the upper room, but the boy in my fiction succeeds only in tearing out the hair from the young woman's scalp, leaving it white and exposed. In the second of the two scenes described as amazing, the same boy, now several years older, imagines himself as swimming one evening from the coast near his father's farm out into the ocean, where the passengers on a brilliantly lit ocean liner dangle a rope-ladder within his reach and urge him to climb aboard. The boy would willingly have climbed aboard but is prevented from doing so by his fear that his old-fashioned bathing costume, passed down to him by his father, would cling to him when wet and expose to the female passengers an outline of what he calls his tool and his stones.

I have never asked my publisher why he described these two scenes as amazing, but I told him once that I read them often for the satisfaction that I get from them. I get a certain amount of satisfaction from reading almost any passage in any of my books and appreciating the shapeliness of my sentences, but a keener sort of satisfaction is available to me when I read a passage full of meaning.

A thing has meaning for me if it seems connected with another thing, and a work of fiction acquires meaning from the connectedness of its subject-matter. This is a topic that demands an essay of its own, and all I can do here is to point to some of the many connections in the two scenes, as I've called them. Whenever I read that the boy beside the liner sees the painted lips of the female passengers as resembling tomatoes or beetroot, I recall at once the narrator's report of his being repelled by the sight of the salads being prepared in the kitchen of the house where his girl-cousins so often arouse his interest. The brightly lit liner on the ocean at twilight is described as an oblong glow, prefiguring the oblong blur that represents his deity for the clergyman mentioned later in the book and reminding me of the influence of religion in the lives of many of the personages in the text. The white exposed scalp of the young woman in the upper room suggests to me the shaven or close-cropped skulls that nuns formerly concealed under their head-dresses, and this in turn leads me to the upper room of the former convent where the narrator of a later section searches out the strands of hair from the heads of the girls who had once boarded there. And even more provoking than any of the matters just now mentioned is the boy's thinking of the passengers on the liner in the same way that he thinks of characters in works of fiction.

My usual way of trying to understand abstractions is to employ visual or spatial imagery. I do the same thing whenever I try to unravel or explicate the meaning of my more complicated fiction. Perhaps my preference for a certain sort of imagery governs my choice of subject-matter while I'm actually writing, but I'm usually too busy selecting from a welter of imagery to take note of my motives. (I often marvel, long after some or another passage was first written, at references and allusions the significance of which has only just become apparent to me.) Whenever I re-read the pages about the boy and the liner, I contemplate the following. The boy swimming towards the liner thinks of the passengers on board as he thinks of the characters in a work of fiction while he reads it. He would like to join the passengers, just as he would often like to share the experiences of many a fictional character. But the boy who thinks thus is not in the water. The boy is an image-boy in an image-water: a boy called into being by the boy who hurries along the cliff-tops, trying to keep in view a distant oblong of light. And the boy on the cliff-tops is hardly more substantial than the boy in the ocean, having been himself called into being by the narrator of a text titled *Barley Patch*, which was published as a work of fiction with the consent of its author. But this is not the end of the labyrinth, or whatever it might be called. The boy on the cliff-tops, he who might be considered by the casual reader to be a fictional character no different from countless others of his kind – the boy is claimed by the narrator to be a *hypothetical* character, although he, the narrator, doesn't use that word. The narrator of *Barley Patch* claims, early in the book, that he possesses no faculty deserving to be called an *imagination*. Further into the book, the narrator is questioned as to whether or not he has ever wished to be able to report events that he could never have witnessed, the assumption being that his lacking an imagination prevents him from doing so. (I suspect that most readers suppose the personage responsible for the italicised questions to be a version of the implied author, perhaps the same stern version who had overruled his softer-hearted colleagues nearly twenty years before and had caused me to stop writing fiction. I seem to recall thinking thus about the questioner while writing the early pages of my book but then, as the questions become more detailed, I heard them as coming from a personage who is almost always in my mind while I write although she has been mentioned only once in these pages: the Ideal Reader.) The narrator, as part of his answer, gives an account of the solitary boy and his two visions, so to call them. According to the narrator, this account is no part of any work of fiction but a mere summary or outline of a sort of fiction that he himself is not equipped to write.

I sometimes delight in the intricacy and the complexity of the two passages. However, if any reader has seen them as a sort of verbal trickery composed in order to get the narrator out of the corner he has painted himself into, I confess to that reader that I myself come sometimes close to seeing them likewise.

In my earliest plans, *Barley Patch* was meant to comprise no more than twenty thousand words. (The finished work has rather more than a hundred thousand.) The central image that I hoped would generate a network of further images was an image of golden dust-motes swirling in a dark room where a scratched gramophone record threw up the sounds of the song 'O, Dem Golden Slippers'. The fiction, as I envisaged it, was to suggest in a veiled and subtle fashion why I had left off writing, nearly twenty years before, the overly long work of fiction with the same title as the scratchily sounding song and what I had turned to instead.

I've never felt the least interest in the mythologies of my own or any other culture. I tried honestly for my first twenty years to accept the mythology of Christianity but found it of no more value than the episodes from Classical and Nordic mythology that had bored me in my childhood. For a painter or a musician, let alone a writer, to derive inspiration from Orpheus or Leda or their like is beyond my comprehension. And yet, I've drawn strength and meaning throughout my life from a mythology uniquely my own, although for many years

I would not have named it thus. I intend to write more about my private mythology, as I call it, in a later essay. What needs to be stated here is that my usual way of thinking requires me to see my mythology as unfolding in a particular terrain and that I see that terrain as lying on the far side of the terrain where the events reported in my fiction are for ever unfolding. What needs stating also is that I see the terrain where the fictional events of *Barley Patch* unfold as a sort of border district.

I may not have been fully aware of it for many years, but I've always read fiction in order to provide appropriate scenery and personages for the unfolding of my mythology. I became fully aware of what I was doing, and I felt justified for so doing, when I read, perhaps forty years ago, that the personage known as Catherine Earnshaw resembled, or was a version of, a personage in the territory of Gondal. The last sentences of 'The Interior of Gaaldine' allude to this matter, and the same matter influenced me while I was writing many passages in *Barley Patch*. The female personage with the yellow hair and the tilted nose, she who is mentioned near the very end of the book, is a prominent personage in my mythology.

So too is the male personage who might have been a fictional personage enjoying a vision of himself climbing aboard an ocean liner or being welcomed into an upper room by a young female person if only the narrator of a certain work of fiction had been able to *imagine* the personage doing such things.

A HISTORY OF BOOKS

I'm always uncomfortable when I look again at the front cover of my tenth published book. I've been told by persons competent in such matters that *A History of Books* has a well-designed cover, and I believe those people, but whenever I look again at the image of the scowling, middle-aged man that occupies the whole of the cover, I'm reminded of the many occasions when I've struggled to explain to some or another questioner, almost certainly well-intentioned and an admirer of my writing, why I'm truly unable to say how much of any piece of my writing is fiction and how much is autobiography. Sometimes I gave such a questioner what I believed was a thought-provoking answer: I invited him or her to write, at the first opportunity, the first thousand words of an autobiography and then to observe how much of the writing deserved to be called fiction for want of a more suitable name. Sometimes I told the questioner about the complex charts used by Wayne C. Booth in *The Rhetoric of Fiction* to distinguish between such personages as the narrator, the implied author, and the breathing author. At such times, I would mention the descriptive phrase used by Booth for the last-mentioned of those three: *largely unknowable*. 'So, there you are,' I would say, or would feel like saying, to the questioner. 'According to a man who devoted his life to the study of how fiction works on the reader, you are destined never to learn anything of value about me from a study of my fiction.'

Had I ever spoken thus to a questioner in public, he or she would have been entitled, of course, to reply that my being questioned just then involved no scrutiny of any text of mine but was a person-to-person transaction in the everyday world, where people were best served by plain, honest speech. If this hypothetical exchange had taken place after the publication of the first and only edition of A *History of Books*, I might even have had the presence of mind to hold up to my questioner a copy of the book with the image of the scowling man on its cover and, mindful of the need for plain, honest speech, might have delivered something such as the following.

During the countless hours while I've gone on filling the countless pages of the many drafts of my published books, I've never shown to any other persons for their consideration so much as a single page. I can recall reading aloud to my wife occasionally a paragraph that I was especially proud of, but she seldom made any meaningful comment. She seemed to understand that my chief purpose was to hear the sounds of my words spoken aloud to another or, perhaps, to estimate their effect on an invisible readership in time to come. If she was perceptive enough to understand this, she probably understood also that I was not writing for her or for my invisible readership even if I sometimes offered them a choice paragraph for sampling: that I was writing for a personage such as she and I had dealt with often as devout children, when we seemed to be continually in the presence of angels and saints and the three persons of our deity.

Robert Graves's handbook for writers was called *The Reader Over Your Shoulder*, but in the text itself he refers to a crowd of imagined readers whose continual scrutiny keeps the writer from erring or floundering. The author of the long passage quoted in the second-last section of *A History of Books* (correctly identified in the Publisher's Note as Sándor Márai) seems sometimes to have written, and at other times to have wanted to write, for her whom he calls at one time the Eternal and Unknowable but at other times seems to want to meet up with. Booth includes in some of his charts an implied reader. She who supervises most of my own writing I call for present purposes my Ideal Reader, and not in order to conceal her true name but because I myself have no name for her. Being someone obliged to think of all invisible entities as occupying some sort of space, I think of her as being mostly in a far corner of the room where I'm writing, or even in an adjoining room, visible through one or more doors or archways. She seldom looks in my direction, but she is well aware of me. She has a distinctive appearance but she resembles no person that I've actually met. She has never uttered so much as a syllable, but I understand that she is well disposed towards me.

I wrote above that my Ideal Reader supervises most of my writing, but I should have added that she is able to do this without having to be continually present while I write. I understand what she requires of me as one understands the demands of certain silent personages in dreams. I've read none of the work of the mid-twentieth-century American writer James Baldwin, but I read to many of my classes during my teaching years a statement of his: 'Write as much as you can bear to write, and then some more.' I read the statement in class with no comment. I left my students free to suppose what precisely had to be borne, according to Baldwin. I've never felt prevented from writing from a fear of any pain or embarrassment that might follow, but I've had to drive myself time and again to go past what I've supposed was my limit: to try yet again to write the passage truly explaining what I had hoped to explain. At such times, my Ideal Reader often appears. (If she's only a creature of my own devising, well, then, I call her into being.) I know what she expects of me, I know whether or not my latest sentences are worthy of her, and if not, then I must try yet again.

It was my Ideal Reader who required me to begin and later to abandon the twelve drafts of 'Landscape with Freckled Woman' that I mentioned in an earlier essay. It was she for whose sake I spent a whole Sunday in my room in 2008, when I had nearly finished the final draft of *Barley Patch* but seemed unable to make a certain necessary connection. I had planned to make the connection in a paragraph or two during the morning and then to relax at the Hungarian Community Centre in the afternoon. Instead, I had spent the day waiting for an insight that failed to occur. I had in mind all day the claim by Turgenev that his characters first appeared to him in his dreams, signalling their longing for him to write about them. That image had stayed with me for many years, and I was sure I must one day include it in my own fiction. I had in mind for much of that memorable Sunday images of forlorn beings begging with signs and gestures to be admitted to the place they considered their true home. I wanted to admit them to my own fiction, to *Barley Patch*, and yet their being admitted thither seemed certain to violate the complex pattern of meaning that had seemed to be developing during my writing of the almost-finished book.

On the afternoon in question, I had been writing fiction for about forty years and had long since come to an understanding with my Ideal Reader. I would demean us both if I begged her for any sort of favour. I was required to pace the room for hours, perhaps, and to scribble unserviceable passages on scrap paper, but never to compromise. If I stayed true, something worthy of her would find its way onto the page. I might have said, with a nod towards James Baldwin, that I had written as much as I was able to write, and that I would now write more.

The words that I had waited for throughout that miserable Sunday seemed almost to write themselves, so rapidly did they appear on my page. Turgenev's potential characters, as he considered them, were *not* pleading to be written about. The writer had misinterpreted their groans and the waving of their arms. The personages, as I would consider them, wanted only to be left alone: to live out their lives in their own sort of Gondal on the far side of the territory of fiction.

The previous six paragraphs, as I've only just now recalled, were meant to suggest to an inquirer of good will how much or how little of my own story might be found in my fiction, and yet what I actually wrote in those paragraphs seems no sort of answer to any such question. I began the first of the six paragraphs a week ago, and I no longer recall how I strayed or drifted away from what I had meant to write. Even so, what I actually wrote is surely of much value. I believe it to be one of the few passages I've written for publication about a personage who matters much to me. My having diverged thus is a rare event in an essay but it happened often when I wrote fiction. It happened on a memorable occasion while I was writing *Inland*. I had for long seen in mind an image of a garden bed where grew a certain species of begonia. Always responsive to colours, I felt drawn to the combination of dark-green and scarlet provided by the leaves and the blooms. I had no foreknowledge of what this image would provoke me to write, but its constantly occurring to me and its strong effect on me assured me that I would write much of value. Then, when the time came for me to confront the image and to report what next came to me, and after I had stared for long and in vain at the image of the dark-green and the scarlet, I found myself writing copiously about quite a different image. In a distant corner of the same garden where the begonias grew was an ornamental pond where scarlet fish swam among dark-green water-plants, and although I had never suspected it, the pond was connected with the well in rural Hungary that was the central image of my fifth book.

The question that provoked me to write the six meandering paragraphs might have been better answered if I had mentioned what the narrator of *À la recherche du temps perdu* calls *le moi profond*. I've mentioned this entity often since I first read about it. I've called it the Deep Self without ever having felt comfortable about that name. Mention of depth too often suggest the Unconscious, the existence of which most people seem to accept but I consider unproven. I cannot bring myself to think of the mind as a sort of mineshaft. My mind appears to me as extending horizontally in all directions and usually as a variegated landscape. In recent years, I've tried to avoid any sort of technical or pretentious-seeming term. I say nowadays that the man bearing my name becomes a different person whenever he sits at his desk in order to write fiction or that he becomes concerned with matters different from those that usually concern him. And I could readily add, for the sake of anyone interested, that the events pressing on the man-at-his-desk, so to call him, are such that their precise origin seems to him irrelevant.

The first page of notes for my tenth book dates from July 2007, and is headed 'A Book of Endings'. I don't recall whether or not that phrase was intended to be the title of the work, but my finding it just now confirmed what I've often supposed during the years since I last looked back at my notes: that *World Light*, by Halldór Laxness, was the book that first set me composing in my mind the text that became *A History of Books*. I got further confirmation when I saw that *World Light* was the first book to be mentioned as possible subject-matter. In fact, neither the title nor the author of the book was mentioned. What I wrote in my notes was *The White and the Blue*.

I can't recall just now any one example, but I'm sure that I've sometimes had in mind while writing a piece of fiction, whether short or long, the effect of the ending. (I mean the effect on readers *and* on myself, the author. I write not only for others but for my own spiritual well-being, if that's not too grand a phrase.) The final draft for the book was finished in August 2009, about two years after the first notes were made. (For nine months of that time I did little writing – I was nursing my wife at home or keeping her company in hospital during her terminal illness.) Whenever I thought of the effect that I wanted from the ending, which I did often in order to spur myself on with the writing, I was not sure that I would be able to write what was needed to achieve that effect. It would not be enough to quote or to paraphrase anything from Laxness's text. I would have to compose something of my own and to achieve thereby my own comparable effect. I felt almost, but not quite, up to the task. When I daydreamed of what I might finally write, one item seemed always to be missing.

The published text explains well enough the narrator's concern for the mental imagery that served as the setting for what he seemed to see whenever he read his preferred sorts of fiction and his wondering, while he read the near-to-last pages, how the author (the implied author, according to Booth) would be able to find in the sparse landscapes of Iceland an appropriate setting for his ending.

A History of Books is presented as a work of fiction. The last section of the work consists of eight paragraphs of fiction. I am not at all reluctant to declare that the first six of those paragraphs are as accurate a report as I was able to write in 2008 of some of my reactions while I read World Light about thirty years earlier. I declare freely also that the seventh paragraph is fiction of the same sort. While I was writing that paragraph, I tried to summarise accurately my state of mind at the very time while I was writing the paragraph itself. The eighth and final paragraph is seamlessly connected with the paragraphs before it. The eighth paragraph seems to me one of the most impressive of many impressive endings that I've found for my many works of fiction. When I wrote that ending in August 2009, I believed I would write no more fiction. My wife had died, and I was preparing to leave Melbourne after having lived there continuously for sixty years. All my writing in future would be for my archives, so I thought, and the last paragraph of *A History of Books* would serve as a last grand flourish. Yet, that same last paragraph is fiction of a kind that I seldom succeed in writing.

The last paragraph of the last section of *A History of Books* became, nearly seven years after its publication, the last of my many utterances in front of the last of the many audiences that I had addressed during forty-five years as a published author. That last audience was also the largest by far of the many. Having been warned by the organisers that a goodly number of the several hundred present were hoping, as they said, to 'catch up' with me after the event, I had arranged to be led away to a waiting taxi as soon as I had finished speaking. My hasty removal from view seemed to me and, I hoped, to the more perceptive of my audience a passable enactment of the import of the second of the two sentences in my final paragraph.

That sentence, which comprises nine clauses and a hundred and seventeen words, took hardly longer to write than it takes to be read slowly aloud, but it had been weeks, or even months, in the making. For most of that time, I was in a predicament by no means new to me but frustrating nevertheless. I had in mind an image that promised much if only I could find within it or behind it or to one side of it a detail as yet unknown to me. The image in my mind was as simple and as stark as a daubing done by a young child – a white mountain-peak tapered to its apex against a blue sky. The simplicity of the image was deceptive; I had learned during my many years as a writer of fiction that a simple-seeming image might portend a dense network of meaning. What I had also learned was that such an image seldom yielded its meaning readily.

I no longer recall the moment when I grasped at last the promised meaning, which may not have been conveyed to me in the form of a visual detail but rather in the form of words seeming to sound to me or to appear to me. I was enabled to compose with ease the main clause and the eight subordinate clauses of my faultless sentence as soon as I had understood that white is the colour of paper and blue the colour of ink.

A MILLION WINDOWS

I've written already, in the second essay in this collection, that my usual way of assessing the value of a book is to ask myself how much I recall, long afterwards, of the experience of reading the book. I neglected to mention there a similar method that I've sometimes used, which is to ask myself how often I feel urged to look again at certain passages if not to read the whole book again.

I've sometimes, from mere curiosity, tried to assess my own books using the second of the methods just mentioned. (The first of the two methods is hardly suitable, given that I often remember not so much the published text as early drafts or even earlier notions of likely subject-matter.) I value all my books, of course, but the fact remains that I look most often into the eleventh to have been published, and the passage that I look at most often is the paragraph that begins on page 46 of the first edition, which paragraph comprises three hundred and twenty-four words and is, according to the conventions of traditional grammar, a single, sound sentence. According to the same conventions, that single sentence can be analysed into twenty-one separate clauses: a main clause, of course, together with ten adverbial clauses, five adjectival clauses, and five noun clauses. I mention this because readers with scant knowledge of traditional grammar are apt to praise for their long sentences writers who do nothing more skilful than the stringing together of loosely linked phrases and clauses. The works of Thomas Pynchon come to mind, and also the translations into English of works by László Krasznahorkai and Hermann Broch.

Soon after the publication of *A Million Windows* in mid-2014, a prominent scholar and critic, while reading my book for the first time, wrote on the margin of page 46, beside the paragraph comprising the sentence mentioned, the question 'Is this the best sentence I've ever read?' A year and more later, when the same scholar was visiting me as part of his research for some or another project of his, and after he had told me about his handwritten comment, I opened at once the appropriate drawer from among the filing-cabinets containing my Literary Archive, took out the second of the two drafts of *A Million Windows*, and showed him my handwritten comment in the margin beside my paragraph-sentence: 'This is the finest sentence that I've ever composed – GM, March 2014.' (Two comments are needed. The date of my note was only a few months before the publication of the book, which tells me that I was prompted to write what I wrote during a final reading of my final draft. The sentence itself was written about a year earlier. And while I still consider my long sentence to be faultless, I could wish that I had not included the word *ever* in my handwritten sentence. I decided long ago that few adverbs are needed in prose.)

A year after the publication of my eleventh book, I was commissioned by the editor of *Meanjin* to write an essay on some or another aspect of the craft of writing. The finished essay, which was published in the issue dated Autumn 2016, gave me the opportunity to put on record what I consider the most important of the many findings that I've made during a lifetime of writing and of teaching my craft to others. I gave to my essay the title 'In Praise of the Long Sentence', and the text includes my argument that the simple sentence is the natural repository of meaning: that the connection between subject and predicate, which is the basis of the simple sentence, is the essence of meaning. I do not claim in the essay that a long sentence is inherently superior to a short sentence, but I try to demonstrate the admirable suitability of the long sentence for someone such as myself, who delights in discovering connections between things that seemed previously unconnected and in using compound sentences to arrange for the contemplation of connections-between-connections, so to call them: multiple clauses attracting or repelling each other in surprising ways.

A clause, of course, is a sentence within a sentence: a unit of meaning within an aggregation of such units. My paragraph-long sentence, as with all such sentences of more than one clause, is called in traditional grammar a *compound sentence*, and in my essay in *Meanjin* I distinguish between two sorts of compound sentences: the left-branching and the right-branching. In the first sort, most or all of the subordinate clauses precede the main clause or are situated to the left of it, in spatial terms. In the second sort, the main clause is at or near the beginning of the sentence while the subordinate clauses follow it.

I doubt whether any other fiction-writer of my time has used so many compound sentences as I've used, and even if some such writer has nearly equalled my total I feel sure that my left-branching compound sentences far outnumber his or hers. This is no sort of boast. Every sort of sentence is of use for some or another writerly task, but I've come to prefer, and to use more often than others, a type of sentence not much used nowadays. In my essay in *Meanjin*, I speculate that my preference may be simply explained as follows. During my first ten years, I was closer to the nineteenth century than to the twentieth, and much of my reading was from books written decades before my birth. Writers of that era tended to use many more compound sentences than do writers today, and if many of those sentences were left-branching, this may well have been due to the prevalence in school curricula of the Latin language, in which the main verb is the last word in most sentences. Even today, I still sometimes read aloud for their sonority and the measured rhythms of their clause after clause the works of Thomas Hardy and of George Borrow. (And I composed just then with little effort my favourite sort of sentence: a simple sentence but one in which the subject and the object of the verb are separated by several rhythmical phrases.)

I read somewhere the claim that all of the many published works of Jack Kerouac ought to be considered simply as parts of the one book. On certain occasions, I've wondered whether the same claim might be made about my own books. On those occasions, I've wanted to mention in a conversation or in a letter some or another subject-matter that I recall from my writing. The subject-matter and even, sometimes, a phrase or a sentence from the writing, are clear in my mind, but I'm unable to recall the book in which they were published. The matter is made more complicated by the fact of my having sometimes used the same material, so to call it, in two or more pieces of fiction but with each having a different treatment, to use a word favoured by Henry James. The example that I want to write about here is that of the Heytesbury Forest, only pockets of which survive in the world where I sit writing these sentences but which has been preserved in the form of a vast image-forest in the only world that I'm able to write about.

The first-person narrator of the title-piece of my seventh published book reports the effect on himself as a child of his looking at a painting of a road through a forest. Whatever may appear in the published report, I hereby declare that I often felt as a child, on the few occasions when I saw a part of the actual Heytesbury Forest or on the many occasions when I saw an actual or a painted forest-scene that reminded me of the Heytesbury, as though something of immense importance might one day be revealed to me in such a place. If, from my seventh year onwards, I reminded myself that I had once during that year spent several days with my family in a clearing in the actual Heytesbury Forest, I would have recalled from those several days scarcely anything except my having seen a certain small bird dart across a clearing and my having learned from my father that the bird was a species of kingfisher.

Two matters seemed to me extraordinary when I read again recently about the fictional bird towards the end of *A Million Windows*. The first was that nearly seventy years had passed between the moment when the actual bird (almost certainly the sacred kingfisher, *Todiramphus sanctus*), flitted across my field of vision and the moment when I decided that the image of the bird truly belonged in the pattern of imagery that I had in mind while I wrote the third-last section of the book that I look into more often than I look into any other of my books. The second matter is linked to the first. During all the years while I wrote fiction, I was alert for images that recurred to me. I considered such images as likely to belong somewhere in my fiction. Often, I would begin to write about some or another such image before I had learned anything of its meaning, which is to say before I had learned what other images it may have been connected with. I had been interested in birds since childhood. I had taken note of countless birds and had recalled for long afterwards my sightings of them. The kingfisher had taken my eye for moments only, but its image was imprinted on me more clearly than most others of its kind. Why then, did I never try to make use of that image in some earlier work of fiction?

Something that I haven't mentioned in any of these essays is *power*. When I'm reading a passage of what I call true fiction (a true report of the workings of the writer's mind) I feel the effects of a power such as I feel when I'm playing on my fiddle certain sorts of music. The power seems to come not so much from words of even sentences (notes or even melodic phrases) as from the aptness or the inevitability of the piece as a whole. I felt the same sort of power at times while I wrote the previous paragraph. I ended that paragraph with a question. Whenever I try to answer that question, I feel a sort of power deriving from my eleventh book but especially from the last three sections of that book. I feel as though the published text of *A Million Windows* had existed previously in potentiality for who knows how long; that the potential text had always a power of its own just as the published text has now; and that one effect of this power was to hold me back from trying too soon to render the potential text actual.

Just as remarkable as my seeming not to notice, during most of my writing career, the signalling to me of an image so seemingly ready for a place in my fiction, is my having failed to notice, during the same length of time, the resemblance between the predominant colours of the kingfisher and of a certain dressing-gown that I took note of during my childhood. Never having possessed a sense of smell, I seem to have developed an acute awareness of colours and sounds, and many of the connections that have appeared to me from among my store of mental imagery have done so after certain similarities of colour had taken my eye. (I mentioned in an earlier essay the fishpond and the begonia plants that I saw in mind while I wrote *Inland*.) How, then, did I never notice, during most of my life, that the blue and the silver-grey of the bird matched the colours of the chequerboard pattern on the dressing-gown? It will seem fanciful to many a reader, but I'm prepared to believe that the power of certain mental images may be such as to dazzle their possessor, as it were, and to hide from their possessor the true extent of their meaning before he or she is competent enough to report it in words.

Of all that I'm proud of whenever I look again into my eleventh book, I'm most proud of the narrative framework. The first-person narrator of the work has a good deal to say about different narrative techniques, but I sometimes wonder whether the astute reader of the text can accept that he, the first-person narrator, is capable of devising such a complex technique as I devised for it. *A Million Windows* illustrates clearly a distinction made by Wayne C. Booth but not always so easy to discern: the distinction between a certain sort of first-person narrator and the implied author. No reader could reasonably suppose that the man who wrote the text did so in the building of many windows that he refers to so often. At the same time, no reader is entitled to suppose that the last three sections of the book are a report by the man named on the covers of the book of his having discovered, late in life, that his mother, while hardly more than a child, was the victim of a crime or crimes in which *her* own mother was complicit and for which the perpetrator was never held to account. Therein lies the true power of well-wrought fiction: a man can unknowingly reveal, in book after book, his central concerns but only as pieces in an incomplete pattern. I was moved to write an entire work of fiction after I had read a single paragraph about a nameless woman who leaped into a well on the other side of the world three decades before my birth. The title-piece of my collection *Velvet Waters* contains numerous references to streams or to bodies of water far inland and comes to an end with an image of a bereaved young woman standing among water that bubbles miraculously from a spring far out on the Great Plains of the USA. And if all my books are like Jack Kerouac's in being one vast volume, then somewhere in all those pages I once wrote about a few memorable images from a film of the 1960s titled *The Virgin Spring* in which the central action is the rape and murder of a young woman, hardly more than a girl. I wrote that book, that short work of fiction, and that passage of fiction unaware that all three were merely pieces in an incomplete pattern. In the title-piece of my collection *Emerald Blue*, I wrote at length about the significance to me of various forests and of one forest especially, unaware that all I wrote there was part of the same puzzle. At last, in my seventy-fifth year, I wrote the book of fiction that draws me most often to look into it yet again. The last few sections of that book and, perhaps, the whole of that eloquent work serve to complete the pattern mentioned earlier in this paragraph. I expect never to grasp the full meaning for me, the author of this essay, of certain events that took place in the last few years before my birth, but the nameless author reported, in the last pages of *A Million Windows*, as writing a work of fiction intended to explain certain matters to him — that author is on his way to understanding those matters.

SOMETHING FOR THE PAIN

After the publication of my eleventh book, I began to receive letters from people who seemed to know little about my previous books but had been touched in some way by my memoir of the turf, as I sub-titled it. Many of the letter-writers seemed delighted to learn at last that someone else got from horse-racing what they had thought was peculiarly their own and could not be put into words. One such letter-writer, who lived in the far north of New South Wales, wanted to spend a day in my company at a race-meeting of my choice. Knowing my reluctance to travel, he suggested a meeting at Casterton, in south-west Victoria and a long way from his territory. He agreed to meet me in my home-town on the morning of the race-meeting and to have me drive him the last hundred kilometres and more of his long journey.

My book had been praised by most of its reviewers, but a review from Les Carlyon gratified me more than the warm words of all the others. I had never met Les, who has since died, but I had read and had greatly admired most of his books. I admired him all the more because he was the sort of writer that I could never aspire to be: the writer who looked clearly and searchingly at the world around him; and who read his way through library collections and visited the sites of historic events. (I might say of myself what one of Samuel Beckett's characters said: 'I have lived my life in a kind of trance.' Rather than look at things, I wait for things to catch my attention, or else I persuade myself long afterwards that I actually saw them. As for research, I've been daunted all my life by libraries and their retrieval systems, and instead of delving into history, I merely report what fictional personages choose to believe.) I saw Les often at the races in Melbourne during the years when my wife and I went every Saturday to Flemington or Caulfield or Moonee Valley or Sandown. I sometimes watched him discreetly from a distance. He was always alone when I saw him, and I never saw him with either a pen or a notebook in his hands. All he seemed to do was to stare, and mostly he stared at horses. I never saw him in the betting ring, but true lovers of racing are much less concerned about betting than is the casual racegoer.

Among the most impressive passages of Les's writing are his descriptions of horses. Under his scrutiny, every horse was a distinct individual with looks and mannerisms setting it quite apart from all the other browns and bays and chestnuts in the stalls around it. Early in my book, I had confessed that I had never sat astride a horse and never really looked at a horse. When I had learned that my book was going to reviewed in the *Australian* by the man who seemed to spend half his time at the races staring at horses, I was a bit apprehensive, but I need not have worried. What warmed me most in the review was Les's referring to me as a stylist and his praise for the writing in the last paragraph of the book. I'm fond of long sentences for the multiple connections that they bring to light, but I believe that the length and shape of every sentence is determined by the pressure, so to call it, of the thoughts and the feelings needing to be expressed. I could never put this better than did Virginia Woolf when she wrote that a thought or a feeling creates a wave in the mind and that the breaking of the wave is the falling into place of the sentence. The last paragraph of my eleventh book consists of seventeen sentences with an average wordage of about fourteen. I opened *A Million Windows* just now at a page near the middle of the book and found that the average sentence on the page comprised about forty words. This tells me that I'm willing to write short sentences if I think they're needed. The last paragraph of *Something for the Pain* reports the death of a racehorse and the distress of its owner. I turned almost instinctively to short sentences so that each of the details that I saw in mind (and had seen thirty-five years before at Flemington racecourse and had never forgotten) would impress itself on the reader without the distraction of commentary or description and without being connected to other details. But the differing lengths of the sentences would have resulted also from the difference between the two books. One, a memoir, is written in a style closer to conversation while the other might be said to have for its subject-matter an inquiry into the very nature of fiction-writing.

Les Carlyon had written a long review of my book but had made no mention of the second-last of the twenty-seven chapters, 'They're Racing in the Antipodes'. When I had first read the review, I had skimmed it rather than read it, eager to see what a man so steeped in racing lore would make of my having invented a whole world, so to call it, of imaginary racing. Now, of course, I'll never know. I can't believe that he was dismissive of my strange achievement. Being a highly perceptive person, he could have divined that my including that chapter in the book required some effort and that I was not looking for comments. Or, he may simply not have known what to say. My publisher selected a few words from Les's review for inclusion in the preliminary pages of the later editions of my book. Sometimes, when I look at Les's comment 'an unusual book by an unusual man . . . ' I seem to see Les looking somewhat baffled as he pauses over a page near the end of my book and tries to envisage one of the racecourses in New Eden or New Arcady.

My visitor from Grafton was not exactly voluble either, after I had shown him some sample pages from the two crowded filing cabinet drawers that I call the Antipodean Archive. He had stayed overnight in Horsham and had met up with me soon after breakfast. We had coffee in my rented room at the rear of my son's house while I tried to explain within a few minutes what has taken up most of my spare time during the last thirty-five years. (In a folder at the very front of the archive are more than twenty closely typed pages meant to explain to anyone interested after my death how and why I devised my alternative universe, as I sometimes think of it, and what satisfaction I get from adding to it almost daily. That much will always be available for the curious, but no one will ever understand how the thing works. I've never had the time or the urge to put into writing such things as how horses are allotted to different stables, how owners' racing colours are devised, how fields are selected for the various races, how the betting market is framed for each race, and – most importantly – how the result of each race is determined. These and many other matters are nowhere set out in writing, which means that the whole archive may provide a fascinating spectacle for some curious researcher in future, but no one will be able to add to it.)

My visitor and I spent a pleasant day at Casterton races. Late in the day, we were commenting on the misfortune of a trainer from Mount Gambier who had brought three horses to the meeting only to see each finish second. My visitor then told me about a trainer in his district who had recently experienced something even more exasperating. I straight away began to report a remarkable succession of minor placings achieved by the trainer Frederick Schadel (Peacock-blue, black hooped sleeves and spotted cap) before I recalled that this man was one of the leading trainers at Merlynston racecourse in the southernmost city of New Arcady. I finished my anecdote, added the necessary disclaimer, and was pleased when my companion made no comment.

The township where I live is far inland, and the frosts are thick and the stars bright on winter nights. On a certain especially cold night a few years ago, I paused during my task of recording in the appropriate folder the results of some or another lesser race. I recalled hearing from a lecturer at the teachers' college that I attended in the late 1950s that he could learn a great deal about a person if he could learn what he or she did in their free time, when they were absolved from all cares and duties. I understood on that cold night that I might have been reading some classic of literature or listening to some musical masterpiece. I might even have been spending a summer in Europe, perhaps visiting Marcel

Proust's grave or Emily Brontë's. Instead, I was huddled over a desk in a remote township, studying the results of races and the changing fortunes of personages known only to me. I've sometimes felt just a bit uneasy about this, but I no longer feel thus after having learned from one of my long-time correspondents, a person with outstanding qualifications in her profession, that she regularly consults an analyst and that she spent an hour during her latest consultation discussing archetypal metaphors to be found in a recent dream.

I've never understood what archetypes are, but I've sometimes wondered whether the satisfaction that I get from studying one of my charts showing the finishing order of horses in the Goathlands Cup or the Great Southland Hurdle Race or from studying the last six starts of the filly Festoon (Blue, violet and white hooped sleeves, black cap) or of the gelding Rodrigo (Pale blue, maroon band and cap) is no less than the satisfaction got by a different sort of person from his or her dealings with archetypes. I've mentioned elsewhere in this collection my utter lack of interest in classical or any other sort of mythology. I like to think of the personages and the events recorded in my Antipodean Archive as part of my own mythology. Certainly, the continuous and inevitable expansion of the archive serves to illustrate for me the concept of infinity. I've written elsewhere of my wanting certain books never to come to an end. (This might seem like a childish notion, but my life as a writer and a reader has taught me that my wish is capable of fulfilment.) The archive is hardly to be compared to a book. It more often seems a representation of the mind of the man who first uncovered it, and I've never been able to conceive of *that* as finite. The expansion of the archive, or, more accurately, of the mental imagery denoted by the entries, depends on the occurrence of numbers generated at random according to a process that I myself devised. The numbers come from the pages of a bulky edition of the *White Pages Directory* for Melbourne for 2003. What I can never quite comprehend, but what gives me continuous satisfaction, is that many of the sequences of events on the racecourses of the Antipodes seem largely the result of human planning. Trying to account for this brings on a pleasant dizziness.

Some of the letters that came to me after the publication of *Something for the Pain* were blunt reminders of how little I've experienced of the actual workings of the racing industry, as it's called nowadays: of how much I daydreamed about them without knowing the persons involved. A. R. (Alf) Sands, the man I called a demigod in my chapter about him, did not amass the fortune that would have been a fitting reward for the genius that I supposed him to be. One of his grand-daughters, in a gracious letter to me, described his humble, if comfortable, retirement. He took little interest in racing in his last years. He still rose at around daylight but not to prepare horses to win at long odds. He took delight in his productive vegetable garden.

The letter that most set me back reached me only during the past year. The writer had known nothing of me or my books until someone had found in the chapter 'Mary Christian Murday of the Same Address' clear evidence that she, the writer of the letter, had been on my mind while I wrote that chapter. The substance of the chapter should not be paraphrased. The writing in the chapter is as clear and as moving as I'm capable of. I've always considered that chapter one of the most important in the book, and I've read it often since the book was published, sometimes silently and sometimes aloud, for the effect that it has on me. (Let the previous sentence stand as evidence of the importance of my writing to me and of the purity of my motives. I write in order to understand.) *Something for the Pain* being a memoir, I need not use such terms as *narrator* or *implied author*. Gerald Murnane, in the twenty-fourth chapter of his memoir of the turf, wonders how differently his life might have unfolded if he had met as a young man, hardly more than a boy, a young woman, hardly more than a girl and the step-daughter or the adopted daughter of a small-time trainer at Flemington.

The woman who wrote the letter was a little younger than I. She lived in a neighbouring state, only a few hours' drive from where I live. Details in her letter suggested that her life had been not unlike my own; a bearable mixture of joys and sorrows. She was the step-daughter or the adopted daughter of a small-time trainer at Flemington. She reported several details of her early life much at variance with my conjectured version in the chapter that I set such store by. Perhaps she did so from prudence, but she made no mention of the import of my cherished chapter, let alone of the plain narrative, so to call it. A page or two of handwriting on pages from a cheap writing-pad threatened to do away with a female personage whose existence had been of no small value to me for sixty years.

It hardly needs reporting that a few hours after I had written a brief, grateful acknowledgement to the writer of the letter, the female personage mentioned in the previous paragraph was still alive in my mind.

BORDER DISTRICTS

When I went to bed on a certain evening in mid-January, 2010, my Literary Archive consisted of eleven filing-cabinet drawers. Ten of these contained the material for my published books. (Only nine had been published, but the final draft for *A History of Books* had left my hands and was with the publisher.) The eleventh drawer, which was also one of the most crowded, contained the many fictional projects of mine that had come to nothing and, most notably, the thousand and more pages of notes and drafts for the first sections of my abandoned work, *O, Dem Golden Slippers.* I had moved only a few weeks before to the far west of Victoria after having lived for sixty years in the suburbs of Melbourne. Only weeks before leaving Melbourne, I had composed the last paragraph of *A History of Books* to serve as an ending for not only my tenth book but also my career as a writer of fiction. During most of that career, I had written only when I had felt urged to write. I felt no such urge during the last weeks of 2009, and I expected to feel no such urge in future.

On 31 January 2010, I put a clean sheet of lined A4 paper into the Remington Monarch that my future wife had given me in 1965 (the same machine that I'm using today, in March 2021, for these words) and I produced the following.

About a fortnight ago, and only a few days after my trip to the Penola races, I woke in the very early morning after having dreamed the subject-matter of my eleventh book of fiction (sic). For ten minutes and more, I felt urged to actually write the thing. Then I must have fallen asleep. Later, I felt no urge whatever to write any sort of fiction any more. Today, however, I was tempted for about five minutes to write a shortish book of fiction of about 35,000 words. Its title, which also came to me in my dream, is *Border Districts*, which is also, as it happens, the name of the football team that resulted from the merger a few ~~yeard~~ years ago of the Goroke team and a team from Frances, across the border in South Aust.

While I drive from here to Horsham or from anywhere to anywhere to anywhere (sic) in the Wimmera or the West Wimmera, I take note of houses, I mean farmhouses, especially those set far back from the road. I recall noting some impressive, remote-looking farmhouses this side of the border on my trip to Penola. In the work of fiction, a male narrator, perhaps a widower or a divorcee, has moved to a remote district near a border. He is trying to write a book call *Grasslands*. The accounts he gives of his project suggest that he wants to write a sequel to or an imitation of or perhaps even the original of *The Plains*. At some time during his travels near the border, he dares to visit one of the remote homesteads that he has for long stared towards. The house is occupied by four or five young bachelors. Later, he discovers another homestead occupied by four or five elderly bachelors.

More than these few details I've not yet foreseen. Please God, (sic) don't let me get drawn into the writing of any more fiction.

Sometimes I foresee *BD* as being a continuation of *The Plains*. Sometimes, I see my unwritten book as a debunking of *The Plains*. At other times, I foresee a text so complicated as to be open to six or seven interpretations. The bachelors might have turned away from women in order to write better fiction, for example. The homestead is a front for the truest of all, the most demanding of all writers' workshops/retreats. If so, then the elderly blokes are drying out — trying to give up fiction-writing.

In my present mood, I feel tempted to have a go at writing *BD*. If I wrote a hundred finished words daily for six days each week until mid-January of next year, I'd be there.

Yes, why not?

In the first section, I mean the very few first pages a fictional chief character

. . . but why don't I just start writing the first hundred words on this very page?

Two years ago, when I first arrived in the border districts, I guarded my eyes. Perhaps I should explain how I came by that odd expression; how I first learned to think of the faculty of vision as a possible cause of harm.

I got some of my schooling from an order of religious brothers, men who dressed each in a black soutane with a sort of white celluloid bib at his throat. ~~I learned only a few years~~ I read by chance last year, and fifty years since I last saw anyone wearing such a thing, that the white bib ~~is called a rabat~~ was called a *rabat* and was a symbol of chastity. ~~I brought no dictionaries to the border dictionaries, and so~~ Having brought no dictionary to the border districts, I have no way of learning the etymology of the word *rabat*, but the reference to chastity ~~I could never doubt makes perfect sense.~~ seems apt.

All of the above has been typed and fills most of the A4 page. Also on the page are the following sentences and phrases, handwritten in red, which was the colour I used to record useful-seeming thoughts that occurred to me while I was trying to write some or another draft. Whenever I made a note in red, I hoped I would later look back at the note and derive from it further subject-matter.

> Is the homestead dedicated to living as Plainsmen?
> junior seminarians
> Galong – old squatters' houses
> Sacred Heart
> They saw old faming districts from a distance

Reading these notes today, for the first time in more than ten years, is the latest of many similar reminders for me of the fallibility of memory. I've told a number of inquirers that I first thought of writing *Border Districts* after I had woken from a dream about stained glass. Maybe my original dream included images of stained glass, but if so, they could hardly have impressed me. References to coloured glass abound in the final text. If I did not first dream about the stuff, then the many fictional mentions of it can serve as an example of the importance of what I see sometimes from the sides of my eyes or, rather, what sometimes forces itself to my notice from that quarter. (I can recall at least one reference in the final text to eyes that look aslant. When I read that reference today, I was made aware that to look sideways might be considered a way of guarding one's eyes.) During my first months in this far-western township, I walked each day past a small church. At the time when I usually passed, the daylight was such that neither of the two windows nearer the road showed more than a hint of colour. I felt at first hardly any interest in those windows. The importance of coloured glass in my thirteenth book could fairly be said to have resulted from a few mere glitters of tinted light having ambushed me, as it were, from an unlikely quarter, and this sequence of events justifies my long-held policy of never going in search of subject-matter but of trusting instead that my subject-matter will come in search of me.

I am not one of those who take much interest in dreams and their interpretation. Dreams are hardly mentioned in my fiction. I sometimes record details from a dream in my Chronological Archive, but not with any hope that I'll learn something of importance. *Border Districts* is the only piece of fiction of mine that owes anything to any dream of mine, and I've sometimes pondered on this.

While I've been re-reading my books of fiction, sometimes for the first time in decades, I've often found myself seeing in mind not the image-place or the image-person mentioned in the text but the image that I had in mind long before, when I set out to write this or that passage. Sometimes the two sets of images appear to me alternately, in rapid succession. Occasionally, I seem to be seeing both sets of images closely aligned like the two frames of a nineteenth-century stereoscope. *Tamarisk Row*, which I wrote more than fifty years ago, provides me with obvious examples. The sight-in-mind or the sound-in-mind of the words of the title bring to me image after image of the boy I suppose myself to have been in the mid-1940s and of the humble furniture in the room where I sometimes rolled some of my glass marbles around a faded mat. The same mental items bring to mind also even more numerous images of what I insist on calling a fictional personage: a boy, so to call him, more clearly defined than his counterpart; a boy able to do what the other boy could never do, which is to endure as a changeless personage or presence in the mind of some or another faithful reader.

But nothing in my sort of fiction is simple, and this has turned out to be one more essay that raises questions rather than explains. About three quarters of the way through the text of *Border Districts*, the narrator reports his having heard a radio interview with a certain writer. He reports much and speculates much about this writer and her project, which is to discover, in an isolated retreat-house and with the help of other like-minded writers living under strict conditions, the true source of a certain kind of fiction. *Border Districts* is one of the least planned of my books. When I began to write it, I knew little of the complex subject-matter that was soon to offer itself. Of all that subject-matter, the search for the true source of fiction was probably the least expected. (I recall my thinking sometimes while I wrote the early pages that the search for the whereabouts of abandoned *religious* beliefs would be a major theme of the book.) Moreover, the personage most concerned with this search has, I believe, of all the personages in my fiction, the least resemblance to any person known to me in the world where I sit writing these words.

I admit to being guarded and defensive when comparisons are made between the personages in my fiction and actual persons, but I have nothing to hide. Again and again while I've written, I've seen in mind the features of a face or a group of persons around a table and have then gone on to report words or behaviour that I've never witnessed. Many another writer would surely bear me out. This being so, I marvel at the unexpected arrival towards the end of *Border Districts* of a personage I fail to recognise. Where did she come from?

The question bothering me as I write these paragraphs is the same sort of question that drives my fictional personage to outlay a large sum for a house of amber-coloured sandstone with coloured glass in its windows where she and a select group of writers can finally discover the true place of origin of the images of fiction. Where does she come from? She appeared to me readily while I was writing about other matters and had no immediate need of her. I recall that clearly, although I've forgotten much else from the year 2010, when I wrote *Border Districts*. From the moment of her appearance, she seemed possessed of all the qualities and complexities of an actual person. Some of these, such as her interest in Quaker spirituality, would have made her company tiresome to me if she had been an actual person, but others, such as her interest in Richard Jefferies, might have engaged me; and her lack of interest in certain types of fiction was identical to my own. The implied author writes a long letter to the fictional woman from across the border. He does not disclose to his readers the contents of this letter, although he reveals that the contents of one of the drafts of the letter cause him to cringe whenever he re-reads it.

If I know that author, what makes him cringe is no sort of romantic declaration but rather a passage made up mostly of long compound sentences and revealing more than he ought to have revealed about himself.

I freely admit to re-reading certain passages from my books simply in order to be impressed by them and to find in them more meaning than I had previously found and much more than I had been aware of while I first wrote the passages. The last nine lines on page 54 of the first edition of *Border Districts* comprise one such passage. Sometimes, like the implied author of my book, I feel while reading fiction as though I know what it would be like to know the essence of a person. (This is a mere paraphrase and a simplification of my text.) And sometimes, like that same author, I feel as though the part of me that thus feels is my own essence. (This is another paraphrase and simplification.)

After I had first written those lines on page 54, I found and copied the statement by George Gissing about the superiority of fiction over biography, just as the implied author is reported as having done. I clearly recall what next took place. I had always intended that *Border Districts* would include one or more passages about the human eye and even a passage reporting the pressing of a coloured glass marble against a human eye, but I had given no thought to the question of where in the text those passages should occur. I had not handled my biography of George Gissing for at least a decade and had forgotten that one of the items on the dust-jacket was a black-and-white reproduction of a photograph of the author posed so that her eye was strangely lit. While I looked, for the first time in years, at that image-eye, I was surely ordering already in my mind the impressions that I would soon report in a passage of more than two thousand words connected with the passage about the essences and no less impressive than that passage.

So, mere chance delivered to me, in an opportune hour and from an unlikely quarter, the very ingredients I needed for an impressive passage of fiction. Was I, rather, after fifty years as a certain sort of writer, skilled enough to link together in an impressive passage what might have been of no use to another sort of writer? Or, is what we call actual a vast fictional text that we can only sometimes interpret and, even then, only in part?

GREEN SHADOWS
AND OTHER POEMS

Most of the significant events of my life have taken place within a scalene triangle having as its apices the cities Bendigo, Melbourne and Warrnambool. (Another sort of person might consider my having moved to the far west of Victoria after living for sixty years in Melbourne as some sort of aberration, but my fondness for spatial imagery and my lifelong interest in such notions as randomness, potentiality, and predestination led me one day to discover that the bisector of the angle formed by a line from Warrnambool to Melbourne and a line from Bendigo to Melbourne passed neatly through the dot on the map whither I moved in my seventy-first year and where my ashes will lie in due course.) The images in my mind while I wrote *The Plains* owed little to any memories of mine, but I've for long believed that I first became interested in mostly level, grassy landscapes on the one or two occasions in the mid-1940s when I travelled with my parents and my brothers by bus from Bendigo to Warrnambool and when, in late afternoon, between Skipton and Mortlake, I saw an ornate gateway and beyond it, bordered on either side by widely spaced sugar-gums, a driveway that passed from sight behind a distant low hill or led, perhaps, to a dark-green smudge that was a grove of European trees with behind them a glimpse of the upper storey of a bluestone mansion. This was not the only item that went towards the making of a few images that could be said to have obsessed me ever afterwards. My father, the son of a dairy-farmer from the south-western coast, brought home often a copy of the *Leader* or its rival, the *Weekly Times*, both of which served rural Victoria, and I acquired over time from these journals a composite image of my home-state, just as I've since done for many other parts of the world. The pastoralists of the Western District were, during my childhood, among the wealthiest of Victorians, and many families owned racehorses bearing colours dating back to the previous century. Already obsessed with horse-racing, I took these things to heart.

Many years before I was to leave Melbourne, my wife and I and several other couples travelled every May to the celebrated three-day Warrnambool race-meeting. At a certain part of the Princes Highway near Camperdown, I made a point, every year, of staring towards the distant, dark-blue bulge of Mount Elephant, away to the north. Part of the same ritual was my pointedly averting my eyes from each of the brief views of the ocean that offered themselves as we approached Warrnambool. I might have said at least once to my wife, who mostly tolerated what she called my eccentricities, that my ritual was a requirement of the religion that I had submitted to after I had abandoned the religion of my father's family.

I foolishly violated that religion in May 2010. I was a widower recently arrived in my border township, and I was approaching Warrnambool for the first time from the north. When I was near Penshurst, I understood that I was crossing the westernmost corner of my sacred quadrilateral. For the first time in several decades, what I had seen often in mind was within range of my eyes. I had with me the Canon Owl camera that my wife had bought twenty years before, and I drove half-way up the scenic road to the summit of Mount Rouse (100m) intending to photograph the view to the east. Surely every reader of this paragraph has foreseen by now the end of my anecdote. What may not be so readily foreseeable is that my disillusionment came on me only after I had seen what resulted from the development of the film. While I operated the camera, I still believed I was standing in front of my dream-landscape.

'Ode to the Western District' is one of the five poems of mine that I read aloud most often for my own satisfaction. I read it again just now and was reminded yet again that despite my having thought about some or another landscape on every day of my life and despite my having written about some or another landscape in nearly every piece of fiction that I've written, and despite my considering my own mind to be a sort of landscape, I've actually *looked* at very few landscapes and may justly be accused of not having looked properly even at those. Someone was discussing with me once my belief that a single powerful image is able to give rise to a whole work of fiction. He or she asked me if a single such image could have given rise to *all* of my fiction. Without giving any thought to the matter, I described a scene similar to that described in the last nineteen lines of my favourite ode. That discussion took place at least ten years before

I wrote 'Ode to the Western District', and the image of the man in the library would have acquired during that time the details that delight me whenever I read of them, in particular the fact of the creepers and vines on the verandah being so dense that nothing of the immense plains around is visible from the library.

The second of my preferred poems is 'Mrs Balsarini', in which is mentioned a female personage similar to the woman with her back turned in the library. The young housewife in Bendigo is named, but all else about her is speculation and surmise. Whenever I read the last four and a half lines of her poem, I marvel yet again at the remarkable insight of the narrator of À *la recherche du temps perdu*, he who wrote of the *book written on the heart*. If I had never read those words, I might never have written my poem. Nor would I have been half so capable of contemplating the miracle of a man in his eighth decade being able to decipher the imprint on his own heart of the sight of a drawn blind and an orange window-sill all of seventy years before.

The third of the poems is 'Ode to Gippsland', which tells me, whenever I read it, not so much the story of Catherine Mary Murnane, who spent her childhood in Korumburra and whose ashes are buried here, near the South Australian border, but the story of our joint life, which lasted for almost forty-five years and which ended rather well after having several times seemed likely to end far otherwise.

The fourth of the poems is 'Last Poem'. When I wrote it in 2015, I was in no doubt that the last lines of that poem would be the last lines of mine to be published. Even if I had recalled my having thought likewise twenty years before, when I wrote the last lines of the last piece in *Emerald Blue*, and likewise again after I had written first *A History of Books* and then *Border Districts*, I would not have doubted my resolve. I have now, of course, almost finished the second-last section of still another book, but I've had the satisfaction, for five years, of writing only for my archives and of having as my last published item a short, simple poem that boasted not so much of what I had written but of what I had *not* written.

I've read somewhere the claim that a person reveals more by telling what he or she does *not* do than is revealed by a list of deeds or achievements. I don't know what is revealed by my list of the things never to be found in my poems (or in my fiction), but I'm well aware that some of what I've avoided makes up the entire subject-matter of another sort of writer. Many critics have observed this. One wrote, long ago, that the world got left out of my fiction. That claim didn't bother me, but I was annoyed recently to read, at the end of a mostly favourable review of one of my books recently published in the United Kingdom, the disapproving comment that I seemed unaware that a different sort of landscape had preceded the Australian landscape that I wrote about so often and that a different sort of people had occupied that landscape. These are matters that I'm well aware of, but I exercise the freedom enjoyed by all writers in this country: the freedom of choosing what they wish to write about, even if I seldom chose but was more often driven.

During the eight years between my leaving school and my being persuaded by the girl-friend who was later my wife that I ought to enrol at university, my vision of myself in my retirement was as follows. I was a single man, whether a lifelong bachelor or a divorcee hardly mattered. I was alone every evening and free to sip beer while I read or wrote or played an elaborate horse-racing game that I had devised and developed over many years. I lived in the far west of Victoria, in the township of Apsley or, perhaps, in nearby Edenhope. When I indulged in this daydream, I was still in Melbourne. Those townships and the mostly empty districts around them were far away from me, on the other side of what was always known as the Western District and had impressed itself on me as a child. (Any book such as *The Plains* was unheard of then, but I might say now that I was dreaming of finding for myself a plain beyond the Plains.) My career as a primary-school teacher had been utterly undistinguished, but I had drawn much strength for many years from an achievement unknown to my colleagues or even to my few friends: I had had published, under a pseudonym but by a reputable publisher, a moderately well received volume of poetry.

I would need to write another essay to try to explain why I failed to write, in earlier years, the sort of poetry that I wrote so fluently in 2014 and 2015. For about twelve months, I was able to compose stanza after stanza with far fewer corrections and alterations than I've always made while writing prose. And if that were not miraculous enough, I was at the time, and still am, a single man who plays golf regularly at nearby Edenhope and Apsley and who sips home-brewed beer of an evening while adding to his so-called Antipodean Archive.

And no, I haven't forgotten the fifth poem, which is 'Coate Water to Glinton'. Reading that poem aloud enables me to indulge my lifelong passion for maps and landscapes and to acknowledge not only the heroism of one of the few poets that I wholly admire but his devotion to the personage that I think of as his Ideal Reader.

LAST LETTER
TO A READER

When I set out, nearly a year ago, to read all my published books, I fully intended to read every page of the several thousand pages they contain, but I did no such thing. What happened in almost every instance was that a certain page, or even a certain passage, would bring to mind something other than the imagery or the state of feeling that was likely to have brought into being that page or that passage. The urge to put into words my latest insight was stronger than the urge to experience again the earlier, and so I would write rather than read.

Robert Musil wrote somewhere about the baroque palaces erected by the philosophers: vast labyrinths visited by no one. I mentioned in *Barley Patch* the memory-palaces laid out, room after room along corridor after corridor, by thinkers of old for the systematic storage of their most precious mental possessions. I've mentioned in my own writings my perception of *mind* as a sort of *space* the boundaries of which are far beyond my reach, and the image that most often occurs to me when I try to comprehend the significance of the million and more of my published words is of a vast and variegated landscape. (And yes, that landscape is mostly level and seems to adjoin on its farther side the nearest of the landscapes brought to mind by the contents of my Antipodean Archive.)

A History of Books contains within its covers not only the title-piece but three other pieces of short fiction that no reviewer or scholar, so far as I'm aware, has commented on. The narrator of the short piece 'The Boy's Name Was David' claims that a sentence comprising those five words was, of all the countless sentences that he had been obliged to read as a teacher of fiction-writing, the last that he was able to recall. That sentence, which was the opening sentence of a piece of short fiction by a mature-age male student whose name the narrator had long forgotten — that sentence provided me with the title for *my* piece of fiction, and that sentence is one of the two sentences that has most frequently occurred to me during the past few months whenever I've wondered what might comprise a worthy ending to the last essay in this collection. The other of the two is a sentence from the third-last page of the last of the three short pieces under mention, 'Last Letter to a Niece'. (The solitary letter-writer, writing from the southernmost edge of a southern continent to a reader that only he is aware of, is yet another of the fictional personages who bring to my mind the uncle of mine mentioned often in the ninth of these essays.)

No word in any of my fiction actually *describes* anything. I could never hope to describe, even in an essay such as this, my mood as I look back sometimes at the two sentences just mentioned or as I read them aloud, as I often do. 'I have come to hope, dear niece, that the act of writing may be a sort of miracle as a result of which invisible entities are made aware of each other through the medium of the visible.' So writes a fictional personage whose existence I was the first to report to others of his kind. Whenever I read this passage, I feel what I'll call for convenience *elation*.

The narrator of the piece 'The Boy's Name Was David' used the word *exhilaration* to denote or suggest what he had felt when he first read those same words as the first sentence of a piece of short fiction by a student whose name and appearance he had long since forgotten. The same narrator had written, in his own piece of short fiction, 'There was never a boy named David, the writer of the fiction might as well have written, but if you, the Reader, and I, the Writer, can agree that there might have been a boy so named, then I undertake to tell you what you could never otherwise have learned about any boy of any name.'

I've called it *elation* and *exhilaration*, but my state of mind when I see sometimes what my writing has disclosed to me, never mind what it may have meant for others, may be better suggested if I report that I've sometimes, after reading some or another passage of my own writing, composed and played on my fiddle for my own satisfaction some or another melody meant to resolve my own tension or, perhaps, to celebrate that tension itself.

Hol volt; hol nem volt . . . literally 'where it was; where it was not . . . ' These are the opening words of many a fairy-tale in the Magyar, my adopted language. The tension arising from these paradoxical clauses is not unlike the tension that I feel at this moment, as I repeat to myself the sentence about the boy named David or the sentence written by the solitary uncle to his non-existent niece, and as I look for an appropriate ending to what will surely be my last published work. The tension is not at all painful. The tension is a form of energy and can be productive. The tension drove me recently, after I had finished an earlier essay in this collection, to compose the following and afterwards an original melody to fit the words.

Angyalom, ments engem;
Mert fél gyenge testem.
Jön hozzám gyorsan a kínos halál.

Tudom, hogy azután
Vár igaz tudomány,
Végtelen síkság, és örök varázs.

Mégis, vagyok ember;
Húsból teremtettek,
Mely akar maradni lélek mellett.

Segíts, te kedvesem,
Bírni türelmesen
Visszamenetem az én mennyembe.

(Freely translated: Save me, Angel-of-mine; my frail body is afraid; a painful death is coming fast. I know what awaits me afterwards: true knowledge, endless plains, and eternal magic. But I'm human. I was created from flesh, which wants to stay close to soul. Help me, dear one, to endure patiently my going back to my own sort of heaven.)

Dear readers,

As well as relying on bookshop sales, And Other Stories relies on subscriptions from people like you for many of our books, whose stories other publishers often consider too risky to take on.

Our subscribers don't just make the books physically happen. They also help us approach booksellers, because we can demonstrate that our books already have readers and fans. And they give us the security to publish in line with our values, which are collaborative, imaginative and 'shamelessly literary'.

All of our subscribers:

- receive a first-edition copy of each of the books they subscribe to
- are thanked by name at the end of our subscriber-supported books
- receive little extras from us by way of thank you, for example: postcards created by our authors

BECOME A SUBSCRIBER, OR GIVE A SUBSCRIPTION TO A FRIEND

Visit andotherstories.org/subscriptions to help make our books happen. You can subscribe to books we're in the process of making. To purchase books we have already published, we urge you to support your local or favourite bookshop and order directly from them – the often unsung heroes of publishing.

OTHER WAYS TO GET INVOLVED

If you'd like to know about upcoming events and reading groups (our foreign-language reading groups help us choose books to publish, for example) you can:

- join our mailing list at: andotherstories.org
- follow us on Twitter: @andothertweets
- join us on Facebook: facebook.com/AndOtherStoriesBooks
- admire our books on Instagram: @andotherpics
- follow our blog: andotherstories.org/ampersand

GERALD MURNANE is the award-winning author of such acclaimed works of fiction as *Border Districts*, *Inland*, *Barley Patch*, and *The Plains*, as well as the memoir *Something for the Pain*. Murnane lives in the remote village of Goroke in the north-west of Victoria, near the border with South Australia.